Change of Plane

Change of Plane

Albert Marks

ARCHWAY
PUBLISHING

Archway Publishing books may be ordered through booksellers or by contacting:

Archway Publishing
1663 Liberty Drive
Bloomington, IN 47403
www.archwaypublishing.com
1 (888) 242-5904

ISBN: 978-1-4808-2164-4 (sc)
ISBN: 978-1-4808-2165-1 (e)

Library of Congress Control Number: 2015949617

Print information available on the last page.

Archway Publishing rev. date: 10/16/2015

The only thing that is constant is change.
                    Heraclitus 500 B.C.

Plane – a flat or level surface or 2. a level of existence, consciousness or development.
                    Webster's Ninth Dictionary

The view from airplanes to ground evokes fresh visions, new ideas and altered perspectives of commonly held and ingrained thoughts.

CONTENTS

CHAPTER 1.

Home Grown

Southern Minnesota – summer of 1964.

ach life-story has a series of beginnings—birth, baptism, first day of school, first lion kill for an emerging young Masai warrior, and so on. But today was a unique, essential beginning for Mark.

Sitting alone on the curb bordering the precisely mowed and brilliantly green grass of his home's front yard; an awareness of an impending future emerged as in a daydream, but more definite. This awareness cut deeper than the dread of mowing the lawn (a duty performed by him, always on Saturdays and at a jogging pace just to be finished).Mixed with the smell of fresh cut Midwest lawns, a slight scent of hot asphalt and the visual heat waves rising from the street; a new and vivid perspective cut into Mark's idle consciousness, spurring both a firm conviction and blueprint for his adult future.

Suddenly the realization surfaced of a greater and more promising place outside of this small, agricultural town; where, most certainly, a college education would become the essential focus. Call this an innate awakening of this tow-headed, smiling, soon to be fourteen year old, an epiphany from the Lord, or maybe just the confusions that occur in early onset heat stroke; but it would endure as a defining moment and a guiding mission in his life. He was called to move to a more exciting city and savor the challenge of a college education, blended with a rich, rampant campus life ripe with learning, experimentation and an absence of parental supervision. Wow, what a nirvana!

This sweet period of mental drifting was abruptly interrupted by a sudden noise of onrushing cars from both directions, neighbors talking as they walked by and the sharp call from his mother to " get in now for dinner." It was 5:30, the end of the work day, with people returning home and his family dinner was nearly ready – "Yeah, okay, mom."

Sigh. The visionary mood was now broken. Mark's attention shifted to a more basic level. Tonight was meatloaf night and he loved those fried potatoes and onions. Now his stomach was taking precedence over the brain, nothing but a common occurrence for an active teenage boy. Put aside for the moment, college days in a big city beckoned Mark, but alas, they were quite a few agonizing years away. However, the awareness was always present. For that dream-goal to be realized, good grades and more savings would be critical.

As a comfortable, middle class family supported by his father (Lloyd) who owned a solo plumbing and HVAC business and mother (Donna) who worked seasonally outside the home in summer months, Mark's family was amply supplied with food, shelter, medical coverage, school expenses and clothing and even a periodic car trip vacation. In Mark's high school years there was even a short period of family membership in the local municipal golf course, fostering the sport that became an ongoing passion for many years of Mark's life. While there were no basic needs unmet, likewise there was little room for college savings and luxury items. This early learning environment about frugal money management defined the essential distinction between needs and wants, shaping an everlasting value in Mark's life.

The small town offered few highlights or cultural experiences beyond the five good sized lakes in the city limits, featured swimming/boating in the summer and ice fishing/snowmobiling in the winter. Snow shoveling was also a wondrous winter exercise feature. Hence, the city motto; *City of Lakes;* located in Minnesota, which is known by the phrase, L*and of 10,000 Lakes.* So, Mark's town – *a city in a land*, vaguely resembled the model town of Lake Woebegon in the imaginings of Garrison Keillor – another, more famous citizen of Minnesota.

Alternately described by online promotional publications as either "a welcome break from travel on US I-90" or "Southern Minnesota's best kept secret!" Mark's town of Fairmont held no special appeal for him and no nagging nostalgic attraction even after decades of forthcoming absence. A particularly unique factoid about this town was that the population had been stable at 12,000 for over forty-five years. Beyond either failures to do a census (not true) or failure to change the highways signs (also not true), we are left to consider an old joke as the explanation. *Yeah, you may wonder, how it is possible that this town's population did not change after all those years Well, every time a baby is born, a man leaves town!*

As soon as high school graduation was completed – in actuality, just a month later, Mark did leave town seeking new adventures prior to college. First of all, Mark and a friend declared their new found independence from school days by embarking on a surreal hitch-hiking journey. Armed only with sleeping bags and the required $20 in cash to avoid a vagrancy violation, they traveled from Minnesota through the Black Hills and arrived in Yellowstone Park three days later.

There they were forced to camp out in the public bathrooms of Yellowstone Park to avoid freezing. It turned out that early summer nights were surprisingly cold for the ill-prepared duo huddling in their small, basic tent. However, Mark and his friend discovered a sweet refuge from the night-time cold by sitting neck deep in a particular volcanic heated tributary stream of the Yellowstone River. Basking in that warm stream was a wonderful luxury, a sort of open air spa that rendered the boys totally oblivious to any potential dangers of nearby wildlife.

The journey culminated with a visit to the famed communal farm areas around San Sebastopol, California. Although Mark loves vegetables, this brief exposure to organic and communal based farming was enough to convince him that he wasn't fit to grow his own and that the full-blown hippie culture was not his "bag."

During Mark's youth, the town economy was based on agricultural products and high yield farming. The rich, black fertile dirt there is renewed by a deep and prolonged frost. There was also a large national canning factory and a regional plant for the then developing company, 3M. Historically, the town was founded as the county seat in 1862 and prospered in the mid-1930s with an industrial plant called the Railway Motors, world–famous for the singular production of the small, single person, manual pump cars that fit the railroad tracks and were essential in rail maintenance and emergency repairs.(Fig. 1.1). These cars and other industrial products of the plant were key elements in supporting the communal, patriotic war effort of World War II. Many of the town's residents were employed here, including members of Mark's family; his mother, granddad Willy and Uncle Chuck.

In more recent history, two famous people visited Fairmont to promote opportunities in commerce and culture of this small community. First of all, Sir Paul McCartney (yes, that one from the Beatles) and his late wife, Linda visited with much fanfare to inspect the agricultural plant that they had contracted with to produce a specialized line of natural food products. The second famed person, the American realist landscape artist, P. Buckley Moss, befriended a local art dealer Lisa Dahl and for several years, made time to visit her shop called *On the Wall*. And in retrospect, it stands as a fairly amazing fact that one of the most famous musicians of the twentieth century and an outstanding artist would choose to honor the town with their attention and personal visits.

From the first day (as he forgot his immunization papers and packed lunch), Mark's fourth grade experience was a rocky road. Not the ice cream type, but the driving for fifty miles at night with bad shocks and dim headlights on a rutted, rural gravel road in a dense fog type. Mark's teacher, Mr. Ferguson, was a small, wiry, intense dynamo who tolerated no deviation from perfect order, maximum effort and impeccable classroom performance. These values were an icon of virtue for a teacher, but a nightmare for a misbehaving, misunderstood and low achieving student, like Mark. School just seemed to lack significance for him. Gym class was fun at times, but that was pretty much the only important part of the school day for Mark.

In that era, classrooms came with blackboards (vs. today's white) and the white chalk was removed with two foot long erasers. Mr. Ferguson habitually waved the erasers to emphasize key points of instruction, frequently adjusted his black horned-rimmed glasses and occasionally pointed threateningly at misbehaving students. Furthermore, he and periodically bopped some particularly inattentive students on the back of their oblivious, sleepy little heads.

While it could be debated (only by Mark) that Mark's school performance and obedience were woeful, it could be interpreted that Mark was simply having fun with socialization, chatting and generally playing hard in outdoor recess periods. Following an episode when a girl classmate's glasses were knocked from her face by an awesomely vigorous throw in gym class, Mark was sent to the principal's office to chat with Mr. Derrick, whom he came to know rather well in the next three months. Mr. Derrick was a kind enough soul, always well dressed in a suit and tie (a style that Mark admired) and certainly understood Mark's dilemma of extra energy and perhaps, lack of concern with grades, home-work, class projects or the importance of quiet attention in class.

The situation culminated in a mid-year meeting with Mark's dad, Lloyd, (known to all as Shorty because of his five-foot seven stature), Mr. Ferguson and Mr. Derrick. Quickly noting that all three men were seated around the principal's desk with their arms crossed, Mark crossed his arms also, receiving an immediate scowl from his dad and a knowing smirk from Mr. Ferguson. While modern psychologists claim that teenagers tend to lack the ability to accurately analyze emotional states in others; Mark could tell this wasn't going to be good. And besides, he was out-numbered and cornered in this small office. Mark recalled hearing negative language to the effect that he was "going to be held back if he didn't improve his grades, his attention and his attitude".

The previous week, Mr. Ferguson had totally loss control of his precise demeanor and had thrown his favorite eraser at Mark, who nonchalantly caught it left handed a mere foot in front of his face. So far during the meeting, Mark had been quietly listening to the criticisms and warnings of the meeting with wide, concerned eyes but finally blurted out in desperation; "But dad, it's not fair, I wasn't doing anything, just sitting at my desk and he (Mr. Ferguson) threw his eraser at me!!!" Shorty countered quickly "You probably deserved it." Then he abruptly addressed the school officials and added "I can say that we will get this straightened out at home and things will improve. Thank you both for your time."

Standing quickly and excusing himself from the heated office, Shorty left and Mark fully realized he now had no allies and was truly in deep trouble. Oh,oh,crap ! he fretted. Mark knew he was in for probable punishment at home, maybe even having to mow the lawn twice a week and no television.

But alas, there is no time to dwell on this bad situation. Living in Minnesota, you learn to avoid self pity, to be stoic and project a smooth layer of cheerful, low-key humor (ahem, sardonic comes to mind in other regions).To para-phrase the Minnesota lyricist Garrison Keillor; "in defense of comedy it gives good value." To endure the six months (or so) of winter torture: gray skies, too many clothes, wind, ice and snow; you learn to enjoy snowmobiling, ice fishing and of course, hockey. For the non-athletic citizens there is also the ever-popular snow shoveling as the prime outdoor activities. A reasonable question might be, *"How can anyone endure this?"* The communal, stereotypic an-swer to the winter question was, *"Oh, you get used to it!"* Very perplexing, that answer, isn't it?

Certainly, these facts were the basis of Mark's life-long disdain for winter woes. Mark admittedly had difficulty coping with winter.

That feeling of accommodation to winter weather is beautifully envisioned by the image of the actress Frances McDormand, as the pregnant sheriff in the movie *Fargo*. The movie was based on a true story, set in part in Minnesota. Early in the movie she stares into the limitless, frozen prai-rie, surrounded by a stark, diffused gray sunlight and buf-feted by a heavy wind. Her simple response to her deputy about the intense weather is, "Yup, it's going to be a cold one." Wouldn't that same observation have been as effective from the heated comfort of her SUV parked nearby?

Coping with the throes of winter produces a micro-cul-ture of well-worn warnings. For example: let your outside faucets drip, put a flag on your elevated car antennae, don't park on the street after a snow storm (your car may well be trapped by the early-morning snow plows) and don't wash your car in sub-zero temperatures, persist as some of the most reliable and useful axioms. But a couple of warnings for children seem most entertaining. The classic advice, "don't eat yellow snow," probably explains the lack of popularity of pineapple flavored snow cones and makes perfect sense. But the peak of nonsense is the old adage, "never put your tongue on a parking meter!" What kind of perverted fool would ever want to do that, anyway? It would only be the adventuresome kid who desperately wants to defy his elders.

Probably the same devious miscreant who makes a game of throwing a rock encased in a hardened snow ball at big trucks as they pass unsuspecting through the downtown district. In fact, that is the very same kid who subsequently enjoys sprinting at full speed around and through snow drifts as the enraged driver chases futilely after him. It seems truly amazing that an older man, generally out of shape and temporarily stiff from excessive time in sitting, can brake a big rig, jump out of a high cab and burst into full speed running effort, all in a matter of seconds.

Perhaps an unassuming, humble attitude toward hardship in all forms, led some University of Minnesota (founded in 1912) founders to adopt the sports mascot name of the Golden Gophers! Now, who would be afraid of a Golden Gopher? For years during and after Mark's college experience he felt that the mascot name might be the weakest, most impotent in the land. However, recently Mark feels fortified and relieved in learning that there may be a weaker mascot name, the Banana Slugs of the Santa Cruz football team. Now most certainly, a Banana Slug would be terrified of a Golden Gopher on the hunt!

Because our English language is so rich with nuance, many interchange-able terms can be used to convey the same topic or event. As a result of the onerous school meeting and subsequent old school, home-style behavior modification, Mark had a sudden awakening of self-awareness (compounded by a sore ass).You may call it an eureka, a revelation, a tipping point or personal breakthrough, but whichever title we may prefer; the light switch turned on and glowed white, stark and hot like an exposed bulb mounted on the ceiling of his being.

Henceforth, grades were to become Mark's Holy Grail. Grades conveyed a level of certain commitment, an undeniable mission and most definitely; an element of family pressure, support and unstated pride. Consequently, the grades steadily improved from grade school into high school. After his freshman year in high school, Mark never missed the honor roll, and graduated with high distinction. Mark regarded this process as instrumental to access into college and enjoyed the additional element of academic competition with fellow classmates (usually the exact same six or seven students) at the end of each quarter. Mark realized that test taking, class-room projects and studying had evolved to his own business process, whereby fun and idle time became secondary pursuits.

Irregardless, Mark truly enjoyed the accelerated English class, with Ms. Janet, who was young, single, blonde, well proportioned and always wore short skirts, which were duly appreciated by the boys when she would periodically drop her eraser and bend to pick it up. So much for participles, adjectives and pronouns; but this was a true, rare socialization experience (or maybe a measure of unrequited lust)! Tragic indeed, that Ms. Janet left the school for Mark's senior year, due to some poorly explained pregnancy issue!

During these formative years, Mark's intolerance of winter cold and the relatively enforced inactivity began to be more and more troubling. No one looks very good in heavy winter clothing and thick caps, with a running nose and an ice moustache. For example, Miss Universe candidates from Russian states seldom merit enough notice to get past the first qualification round. And heading over to the fitness gym was not yet an established norm in that era, so for Mark, high school interscholastic gymnastics served as both a competitive, recreational and fitness outlet. But most definitely, it offered a treasured relief for cold weather woes.

Perhaps, in place of having few friends, Mark also developed a friend in music (but only a treat at night).Huddled under the bed covers to dampen the sound from the sleeping family, Mark rocked out to the burgeoning beauty of rock and heavy metal music. In those days of radio transmission, Mark's prized lime green RCA transistor radio, could clearly pick up only the awesome stations of KAAY (Little Rock, Arkansas),KOMA (Oklahoma City, Oklahoma)and WLS(Chicago, Illinois) with their 50,000 watt night-time signals.

As teenagers grow, they experiment with dress, actions and trials with varied hairstyles that suit their persona; those that express and eventually define their inner self-concept. A lot of mirror time results. For many guys, this process is compounded as puberty hits, causing new dilemmas with facial hair styling. Mark's choice was clear-cut (no pun intended) as he had suffered a minor, but indelible personal trauma as a twelve year old, when his Dad took him to the friendly local, ex-military barber replete with the old-style swiveling barber chairs and out came the ceramic bowl on top of the head and the resulting fast, furious and ludicrous circumferential haircut, known as the bowl cut.

Wise people have claimed that a mark of intelligence is learning from past mistakes and Mark's preferred hairstyle was now simply defined, as long as possible, enduring whatever parental and local societal sanctions would tolerate. In concert with the exploding number of long haired rock bands in the late sixties and early seventies, hair length became a universal symbol of freedom and rebellion, of expression and the signature of a new age. Admittedly, with older Americans (for Mark's peers this was operationally defined as over forty), it became associated and perceived as a degrading stigma of bums and drug addicts, anti-war demonstrators (Vietnam was raging across the national political scene) and all other designated, undesirable societal scourge.

All of this outrage against long hair, stood in sharp contrast to the long-standing traditional hairstyles of our nation's founding fathers; i.e., Washington and Jefferson and spiritual icons such as Moses, Samson (haunted by his regrettable hairstyle decision) and of course, Jesus Christ. Where would these historic men have been with short hair styles? Who knows what we all may have lost with our historical legacies? One can only envision Christ walking among the common man in ancient Egypt with a crew cut, attempting to gather his disciples with the request; "Come and I will make you fishers of men." You can almost hear the resulting laughter, and side comments; "Hey, I ain't never seen no fisher-man with a crew cut, huh!" As years of rejection passed, and the day of the last supper emerged, maybe Christ would have endured alone, and might have been forced to go to the biblical era Denny's with the sad lament; "Table for one, please."

Life as a teenager proceeded with few outstanding experiences; no gang threats, no bullying or vicious personality conflicts and no heart-rending romantic episodes. As a rising junior in summer school; Mark was fortunate to make friends with the ever-lovely, super-popular cheerleader Carla. The time in summer school really paid off for Mark as she unbelievably agreed (she was voted the Mid-Winter Queen) to go as his date to the prestigious mid-winter pep dance!

Man, that dance was good for a ton of social status points. In fact, it was enough to shimmer throughout his senior year, despite losing Carla's affections to a bigger (but assuredly not better) football player. However, there were two notable, outstanding events during Mark's high school years; one from nature and one from musical mysticism; both equally mind-blowing for Mark's emerging rural American, mid-century consciousness.

The term *"mind-blowing"* became an over-used impact term of the '60s and '70s that emerged as interlaced (no pun intended) with the cultish drug usage of that era. This era popularized the use of a cascade of chemicals (LSD, psilocybin, mescaline, peyote and hash) to supplement the ever-popular mary jane, aka marijuana. This torrent of drug use was idealized by mystical druggies, Ken Kesey and Tim Leary and chronicled by Thomas Wolfe in the book, The Electric Kool Aid Acid Test. [1] Consequently, the use of the mind-blowing term seamlessly blended into daily

---

[1] Wolfe, Thomas. 1968. The Electric Kool Aid Acid Test. Farrar, Straus, Giroux. NY.

language; denoting anything that was beyond prior mental and sensory awareness or experience; indeed, something that exceeded even the wildest specter of imagination.

In 1968, the town experienced a tornado, which caused no structural damage other than to the psyches of Mark and neighborhood best friend, Ken while touring a small lake in a Minnesota-made Core Craft™ canoe. What started out as an overcast warm spring day, was shattered by intense gusty winds, compelling the buddy canoeists to begin strong paddling back to shore into a stiff, unrelenting head-wind. Suddenly, the atmosphere calmed completely, replaced by a eerily deadening, pressure filled quiet. Then simultaneously, both Mark and Ken turned to witness what they perceived to be a train crossing the nearby railroad bridge at the periphery of the lake.

WHAM, just as numerous eyewitness accounts frequently describe, the thundering train sound was actually a twister ripping down the lake shore, black and angry, whipping up trees and debris in its path. This image was both eye-popping and mind-blowing, like observing your imminent and certain cause of death. Ken, serving as the navigator and guardian of his father's cherished canoe, begin to scream, *"Let's get the hell out of here. Paddle, paddle!"* Mark yelled back, *"Jesus, that's sooo close! Woo, hoo"* he huffed, struggling for breath with the effort of maximal paddling.

While we are unsure if the Guinness Book of World Records has a category for the fastest two-man propelled canoe 400 meter sprint, but the frantic, furious paddling rate of Ken and Mark might have qualified as a record setting time. Mercifully, the tornado cut a course out into the empty farm fields at the adjacent property to the lake shore, sparing Ken and Mark from ending up in the plains of Kansas, or maybe even worse. From this natural event, Mark's perspective changed. Yes, this was a change of plane for Mark. As the by-product of considerable reflective thought for a teenager, the mind-blowing tornado produced an equivalent mind-expanding concept that persisted for Mark into adulthood. No longer was life an immortal progression. The tornado's threat manifested the realization that life was a finite state that could be easily erased; brutally, rapidly and without warning.

Another equally mind-blowing experience, but much sweeter one, happened just a couple of months later during a rare family vacation trip to Niles, Michigan to visit Uncle Emil's family. Beyond the pure joys of family reunion, visits to the great sand dunes of Lake Michigan and boating trips were planned.

The family outings sounded great to Mark, but his anticipation came with a trade-off, because the final night family dinner was planned at a popular local dinner theater called the *Wine and Roses*. The mere concept of a dinner theater sent chills of dread through Mark, who strongly feared that the musical style of Lawrence Welk would prevail for two hours of—one, and ah two, and ah three type cadence. That thought was enough to evoke an impending nausea, regardless of how awesomely delicious the meal might prove to be.

When the fateful night arrived, Mark was dragged to the event, despite begging and pleading for mercy. As the family entered the restaurant, Mark's frets were intensified, no other teenagers or children in sight, only old people dressed in suits and the ladies in dresses. *Ugh, why ME*, thought Mark. *What about the music stage? Could it get any worse?* Well, a glimmer of hope soon emerged producing a smile on Mark's face as he analyzed the stage set-up. Not only was there a huge, fabulous drum set at the background of the stage, several guitars stood near four microphone stands. Even more surprising, the multiple stage hands working around the equipment were long haired, cool dudes and they were tuning up some butt kicking speakers! *No way, could this be Lawrence Welk stuff,* thought Mark with sudden, hopeful relief. This set-up looked just like the rock bands that Mark listened to with such admiration and excitement and well maybe, even the teen-age concept of reverence.

After the first course salad, a manager type guy in tuxedo and slicked back hair (it must be Brylcrème™) emerged on the stage, the lights were dimmed as he announced the night's musical act,

"Ladies and gentlemen, our heartfelt welcome to this special night here at Wine and Roses. We couldn't be more proud to welcome our group here, direct from Chicago and the Roosevelt Music University .Tonight, for your enjoyment, we have a brand new band performing their all original music, now please welcome the <u>Chicago Transit Authority</u>!!"

Boom, the group walked onto stage, long hair and cool dress, one by one and two by two, they chose their stations. *What is going on here? A band with eight members,* how weird thought Mark, accustomed to the prevailing four or five member rock bands that he loved. Even more odd, some of the band members were carrying brass horns, *and what is that about?*, stimulating further wonder for Mark.

But then the music blasted out, sweet energy flowing like a river into the audience—upbeat guitars and horns, timed by the drums and a group harmony of singing: *As I was walking down the street one day / a man came up to me and asked / does anyone know what time it is?* This was fantastic music, in a style unheard of by Mark (or even dreamed of); so powerful and so vigorous that it was pure ecstasy! Envision the famed TV commercial for Bose speakers in which the long haired guy is reclined in a comfy chair, while his hair is being blown straight backward while facing the force of the music – that's the precise feeling bursting inside Mark's brain.

Now, another change of plane had happened. Mark (and his family who were protectively covering their ears while frowning due to the music volume) was witnessing the breathtaking introduction of the very first paid gig of the forthcoming super band called *Chicago*. Immediately after the dinner and show completion, Mark dashed up to the stage exclaiming to the lead singers (Robert Lamm and Terry Kath);

"You guys are fabulous, that's the most awesome sound I've ever heard. Do you guys have an album?"(these were the old days of large black, scratchable vinyl plastic discs, known as record albums).The band's reply, "Thanks man, we are workin' on an album, so look for it sometime in the fall."

"OK, you know I will !" responded Mark, full of joyous expectation. It was this unforgettable event that fueled Mark's enduring love of both live concerts and most of all, his lifelong favorite band, *Chicago*. It also impressed on Mark a very seminal lesson for his future. Never assume that appearances (or titles like a dinner theatre) will determine the true reality of a person, place or event. The biblical lessons were coming to life in modern form. Or to frame it in other more common terms, if you assume, you make an ass of U and Me.

Likewise, the dinner show galvanized an understanding from a few years prior, when Mark had resolutely refused his friend, Ken's invitation to go see *a damn cowboy movie.* After relenting and seeing the all-time blockbuster, *Butch Cassidy and the Sundance Kid*, Mark fully realized that preconceived notions could be a dangerous and regrettable mode of thought.

However, Mark could not restrain his youthful excitement and exuberance of the singular knowledge that he had witnessed a fabulous new band at it's inception and for the next few months missed no opportunity to tell his friends and anyone within earshot about his amazing personal discovery while expressing his personal prediction.

"This band is so dang awesome and they are going to blow the Beatles right out of the water!" "Just you wait, they are going to have Number One hits and best of all, they are an American band." In retrospect, it's indeed too bad that Mark did not have the vision, chutzpah, money and connections to act as the producer and promoter for the band. Supported by the music business and Chicago's commercial success; Mark certainly had the junior soothsayer role goin' on. As promised by the band in the summer of 1968, in October the first of a battalion of albums to come, Chicago's double album *The Chicago Transit Authority* was released and jubilantly purchased by Mark at his local Sears store.

During the junior year in high school, Mark's extra-curricular interests bridged from his desired sports (the G's-gymnastics and golf) to include a festering desire to write. Recalling his preteen triumph of reading (and comprehending) the entire literary tome called The Good Earth [2], he was rewarded by family amazement that he could recall with accuracy many of the multiple generations of Chinese families within the book. So after some degree of pleading, Mark began to write pieces for the school newspaper, The Echo, a widely read and scrupulously edited (by the principal) publication within the school body and by a few interested parents.(like Mark's) Understandably, Mark contributed mainly game reports articles and an occasional editorial piece.

Powered forward by each subsequent article and suffering from minor delusions of greatness, Mark began to daydream of writing a great and classic book. *Someday I hope to write something so deep, so ass-kicking and so acetone that even Michener and Wolfe will notice and send me a congratulatory letter. How sweet it would be, me, recognized by the masters of the combined word, the lingering thought and the thoughtful analysis of a human vice. Before I bask in the brightness of too much self-flattery though, I must avoid the false pride that the Puritans railed against and follow the Christian ethic of being meek,so,nevertheless, I would achieve a source of personal satisfaction.*

During this era, the Minnesota Vikings football team had been founded as an NFL expansion team (1965) and

---

[2] Buck, Pearl S. 1963. The Good Earth.

had an impressive, early success due in part to the strong, steady leadership of their legendary to be Head Coach, Bud Grant. The head football coach of the high school, Tom Mahoney, also excelled in leading the Cardinals to three consecutive, undefeated regular seasons while Mark was in high school! Both coaches had attended the University of Minnesota and played and lettered in football and were room-mates and friends throughout their collegiate careers.

Upon learning of this friendship, Mark surmised that he might avail himself of the two coaches' personal connection, and decided to ask the high school coach if he would be willing to arrange for Mark to interview the Vikings coach, Bud Grant, as background for an article for the student newspaper. While Mark half believed that he would be rejected by Coach Mahoney and more fully believed that if the request was actually made, that Coach Grant would then decline, he proceeded to summon the courage and made his request to Coach Mahoney.

"Well, Mark, that's an interesting idea, you have there. H'mm, let me give it some thought and I will let you know. Did you clear this with the principal?" Coach Mahoney queried with obvious interest in his voice. "Ah, no, mm not yet Coach" hesitated Mark, emotionally stumbling over his words, and silently regretting this apparent oversight of protocol. "OK, then Mark, I will have an answer for you by Monday," the coach responded. "Thanks for your time, Coach." Mark exited the coaches' office, filled with hope, but still anxious about his breach of protocol.

While conceived as a pretty good guy, Coach Mahoney had served as Mark's math teacher in the past and was a stickler for precise details. Furthermore, in his dual role as athletic director he had routinely teased Mark and fellow teammates about his gymnastics being less manly than football. In fact, Mark's friends on the football team frequently razzed him about "jumping around in his underwear" (male gymnasts perform in shorts or tights) and challenged him to come out and practice football with them to see if he could survive.

Being fully emboldened by trash talking challenges or fun-loving insults and always up for a cutting response, Mark would quickly counter with the proposal that he would gladly do the football practice only if the suspect football player would reciprocate and join him by completing a full gymnastic practice session, participating on all the seven specific events. *What a spectacle it would be to see a two hundred-twenty lb, buffed and inflexible football player swinging on the high bar or doing a double-back flip on the floor,* grinned Mark, chuckling at the visual thought. Virtually with no surprise, no football player ever delivered on their end of the challenge. During his junior and senior years, Mark never faced that challenge again (dang football wimps, anyway)!

Much to Mark's joy and amazement, he was called to Coach Mahoney's via the fifth period intercom paging system and was told that he was going be granted a one hour interview with the Vikings coach, Bud Grant, at their off-season training site at Mankato State College in nearby Mankato, MN.

"Now, Mark, he is a busy man, and you need to be organized for the interview and you have just one hour. So, don't screw this favor up, be on time and have your questions ready, do you understand?" counseled Coach

Mahoney assertively. "Yes, sir, I will be prepared, and I thank you for this chance." replied Mark beaming with unrestrained excitement in his eyes. "Great!" "Also, Mark, I spoke with the principal about this and we have agreed that he will have the first shot at reviewing your article before it's printed. Yes?" "Yeah, I guess that's OK." replied Mark with a hint of reservation, struggling with his true feelings. *So, whatever happened to freedom of speech and wasn't this like censorship?,* pondered Mark, yet still overjoyed with the opportunity to interview an NFL coach.

When the vaunted day arrived, the excitement of the scheduled interview was exceeded only by the warmth and low-key personality of Bud Grant as he freely answered and elaborate details on all the scripted questions that Mark posed. Although Coach Grant was generally perceived as a stern personality, there were junctures of shared and relaxed humor during the interview. Coach Grant was reputed to randomly walk into the training room after practices and when seeing rookies languishing in the whirlpool would brusquely announce; "You can't make the club in the tub!" as he quickly exited.

The interview seemed to flash past and when Mark realized (damn it) that he was now fifteen minutes overtime, he quickly apologized for this gaff and thanked the coach by mustering his firmest handshake. As Mark exited to the parking lot, he felt just slightly dizzy from his concentration and accomplishment. *Man I just a spent an hour with the Vikings head coach, are you kidding?*

The resulting interview article easily wrote itself, was approved by the school officials and appeared in the <u>Echo,</u> a week later in the main hometown paper and then, amazingly, was also reprinted in the big-city Minneapolis newspaper; the Tribune. The whole experience was a dizzying victory for writing skills for Mark. Wow! He was now fully convinced that he would pursue an English major at college when the time came.

Furthermore, this personal experience with the head Coach of the Vikings, firmly emblazoned Mark as an enduring, loyal and avid fan of the Minnesota Vikings football team. NOT rabid, however, because that raises thoughts of drooling and thrashing and biting behaviors, which are certainly not Mark's style. Despite the heights of fine winning seasons, the miserable disappointments of Super Bowl losses and more recent poor seasons, Mark is always thrilled to see the Purple and White uniforms take the field to do battle. Like many other loyal fans, Mark is fueled by the fond imprints of the devastating defensive line play of the Purple People Eaters and the scrambling, hi jinks of their prolific quarterback play of Fran Tarkenton. Therefore, all expectations of future seasons are spiced with the remnants of those dominant teams and special players and the sincere belief that they will re-incarnated someday. Hopefully, anyway!

CHAPTER 2.

Lookin' for Adventure

> Get your motor runnin'
> Head out on the highway
> Looking for adventure
> In whatever comes our way.
> "Born to be Wild"
> Steppenwolf [3]

September, 1970.

"**G**et up, it's time to get going!" yelled Shorty from the base of the upstairs bedroom stairwell. *Oh god*, thought Mark, so early, *what time is it?* Mark turned to the alarm, yup, 6:30, it is time to go. Time to go to college, hooray, it's the day that I have dreamed about and strived for and did all that summer work and saved the money instead of buying a car. Today is that day envisioned on that distant hot, shimmery summer day in the past. Vibrating like a dream, a vision, a harbinger

---

[3] Steppenwolf. 1968. Blank Records.

that was happening **today** !!! Wake it up, buddy, it's show-time.

"OK, Dad, I'm moving now." Having served in the Air Force in WW II, Shorty was driven by timely execution of plans. Besides, the long drive to the college – St. Cloud State (in the city of the same name) was weighing heavily on his mind as he thought about the day forthcoming, and just maybe a little nervous about leaving Mark at his new dorm room and new life. Driving wasn't his concern, he had worked several years as a long distance truck driver and he enjoyed driving, today, in the four year old black and white Ford Galaxy with new tires and a fresh oil change. Of course, this trip was thoroughly planned in great detail for months in advance.

Shorty's real worry today was how his wife, Donna, was going to handle this emotional (for her) five hour journey following this unusually early morning wake-up call. She tended to stress out on this stuff, you know, sending her first born away from home without his parents for a prolonged time period for only the second time. A residential, one-week church camp in the summer of 1966, was the only other time, and that was fraught by Mark's swimsuit being lost, one of his shoes being stolen ("no Mom, I swear I didn't lose it"), his bed being short sheeted by all of the older cabin mates and being late for structured art class because he was skipping stones unsupervised on the main dock at the lake.

Donna was worried about Mark's laundry (how was he going to do it alone?), his grades (was he going to start drinking and carousing at night?), and his nutrition (was he going to eat his vegetables?) Maybe though, she was really worried that Mark's new life would leave her neglected, or worse, forgotten. Consequently, a quiet but pervasive layer of tension was riding along in that Galaxy like a thick humid blanket, covering both Donna and Shorty.

Mark, however, was jubilant, strangely relaxed and excited.

"OK, Mark, check the trunk here and see if we got all your stuff, if it's not in there, we're not coming back for it!" Shorty proclaimed with urgency and yelling into the house, "Donna, it's time to get going." "Yes, I'm just getting Jerry ready for school and I'll be ready."

Jerry, the solitary sibling was the younger brother by four years and was today a rising freshman in high school; just like his older brother, Mark also a rising freshman. Today was also a big day for Jerry. Not only was he starting high school, he was getting rid of his brother for awhile. Jerry considered that he would benefit with no brother to harass him, but admitted to himself that there was a trade-off; he was now ensnared as the sole mower of the lawn. Yuck!

Upon arrival in St. Cloud the early fall air was cool, yet heavy with the scent of leaves and ripe with anticipation for Mark (both positive and exciting).But for Donna the day was full of negative and fretful thoughts. Entering the campus it was time to put all thinking aside, because the magically awaited moment was here! College life was beginning for Mark. The check-in procedures to the assigned dorm room, review of orientation paperwork and the process of unloading Mark's sparse clothes and supplies were accomplished in a flurry .It was time for the parents to head back for the return trip and leave Mark in his new adult setting .In departing, Shorty was anxious to get back on the road for the long drive home and merely advised;

"Study hard kid, you can do it."

However, Mom was having difficulty finding any words; her emotions welling up to a painful point, despite all those sleepless nights thinking about just exactly the right, touching speech to deliver. Now as she struggled with the perfect balance of encouragement and precaution, all Donna could muster "aren't you going to kiss your Mom, goodbye?"

Mark leaned into the passenger window, gave Mom a quick, light kiss on the cheek and trying not to show any sadness, uttered quietly, firmly and abruptly "Hey, I'm going be all right, don't worry, Mom." Mark noticed just a small nod from his Mom, really unlike any previous cue he had ever seen from her before. As kids grow up, they certainly encode their mother's expressions: of love, of anger, of concern, pride or disapproval. This gesture, however, was a new expression and was puzzling Mark, momentarily. As they drove off, Mark waved goodbye cheerfully and he noticed his Mom's tears, as a Kleenex™ was brought quickly to hide her face. Mark's feeling of joy in the moment was tempered by his mother's melancholy and distant reaction.

It has begun: the childhood dream of college, envisioned in that eureka moment on the curb, seemingly a lifetime ago. Now the new realm begins: independence, self-reliance and self-discovery and oh yeah, we can't forget the grades! Two hundred dollars in my billfold, a crying Mom, a campus map and geez, "**I'm on my own.**"

Now here Mark is, not of drinking age, looking for dates and partying (a critical recruitment fact about this school was the four to one/ girl to guy student ratio,) no car, and minimal funds. And immediately, the process of adjustment has begun; everything new, unfamiliar and a touch daunting (naw, just thrilling) and Mark's new theme song, *Born to be Wild* is pulsing in his mind. Years later this song was designated as a top fifty rock song of all time [4] and is also credited as inspiring the concept label of heavy metal music by it's lyrics. [5] The song engendered images of black leather, raked forks, windy freedom and delicious rebellion. Back to the imminent present, Mark thought, *I'm getting awful hungry and where was that campus dining hall located, anyway?* Once again, the stomach took precedence over serious thinking.

A basic human need, socialization, is absent in isolation and friends become vital, even more intensely so, without the nearness of family. Hence, beside the demand to make the grade in the classroom, making the grade with new, fellow freshmen (and importantly, fresh-women) became Mark's new goal and quest. Within several days, employing an unbeatable combination of openness, inquisitiveness, solid memory for details and unending chatter, Mark had met and acquainted himself with a host of folks in his classes, in his dorm and even unsuspecting strangers on the campus streets. Many of these unsuspecting strangers would become Mark's friends; sharing in the fun and escapades of crazy college life during the turbulent days of the Vietnam War, student demonstrations, free love and the so-called hippie movement.

---

[4] Vh1 Top 100 Hard Rock Songs. Spreadit.org
[5] Walser R. 1993. Running with the Devil: Power,Gender and Madness in Heavy Metal Music. Wesleyan University Press.

The pervasive campus climate was a daily cacophony of power to the people. The campus scene was filled with long hair, bell bottom blue jeans, the peace sign, weed, women in scant clothing, heavy metal and classic rock music. There was a definite air of revolution or was it, just an evolution? The awesome collection of rock music recorded in the late 60s to early 70s clearly served as the sound track and rally cry of Mark's coming of age generation

For Mark, it seemed that this beautiful music regrettably died in 1983. That signature event occurred when Led Zeppelin, the stalwart icon of the rock culture, released the tinny, pop-sounding ballad called *A Stairway to Heaven* Seemingly, this song broke the code of rock artistry in favor of a streak of rank commercialism. .

Mark's longest childhood friend, Ken, had also chosen St. Cloud State for his education, but was assigned a separate dormitory floor and separate classes, so their time was divided among several new friends in common. That was definitely some good stuff. In an era before co-ed dorms, the primary dorms of the college were named after famous citizens of the local county. The men's dorm was aptly named Stearns Hall, while the women's was questionably and mysteriously named *Holes Hall*. Yes, for real, a fact which always served as the richest joke on campus. In spite of the name, or maybe because of it, Holes Hall was a favorite spot for Mark and his crew and many other guys on the prowl. You know, making new friends is important.

Gradually, Mark amassed a group of regular friends, a crew, consisting of freshmen guys, who mostly came from small rural towns, like his own. If you will, a group composed of members of the tribe. The crew included Dave, tall and thin and studying art and theatre from suburban Minneapolis, Dan, tall, dark haired, good natured from Morton and Greg, short, muscular from his background as a former wrestler and farmer, who studied accounting from Morgan. Interestingly, that those guys from two small towns, Morgan and Morton only a few miles apart but had never previously met until they became part of the crew.

However, the first new member of the crew, Jerry, was a city boy from Minneapolis, who Mark fortuitously met on his first day at school while exploring his assigned class buildings. While both young men were standing somewhat aimlessly on the street checking their class schedules, a look of recognition caused Mark to ask this stranger Jerry,

"Do you have a class here?" "Yea, man, English 101." "Well, so do I, what time is yours" Mark followed. "Mine is at 9" Mark offered his hand in greeting, "I'm Mark, its nice to meet you and it looks like we have the same class!"

Here was a basis of common ground. Jerry responded with a strong handshake, "I'm Jerry. I'll see you in English then. OK, hey I'm going over to the cafeteria and I need to get some lunch before practice starts. You eat at the cafeteria?"

Yet another basis for common ground, thought Mark as he envisioned his brother, also named Jerry. Mark wondered; *How is Jerry doing with the mowing?*

"Yea, I eat at the cafeteria too." How amazing, a third basis of common ground has surfaced. "So, Jerry, what practice are you going to?" "I'm on the gymnastic team here at State." *Now what an amazing series of common ground*, thought Mark. "Hey, Jerry, that is amazing, so am I!!!"

As Jerry considered this news, he studied Mark carefully and queried, "So, man, where did you go to high school?" Mark's response "Fairmont" was met with a knowing nod from Jerry,

"You know, I thought so, I think I remember you now from the State meets, I went to Brooklyn Center and I worked the side horse. You worked floor exercise, I think I recall." And so through the recurrent series of common experiences from this initial random meeting, Mark and Jerry became fast friends with Jerry, now a charter member of the crew.

Being a short, swarthy fellow; Jerry was extremely muscular from years of training to acquire a black belt in karate and training in gymnastics. Additionally, Jerry was special because he owned a car (sort of), a 1960 Chevrolet Corvair with a faulty transmission that required precision shifting and carefully planned parking to avoid all reverse shifting. Despite the new-found depth and breadth of personal independence, Mark still had to rely on his buddies, Ken and Jerry, for rides when critical for off campus trips and errands. When an occasional date occurred, it was always a healthful, safe walking experience. No DUIs here, baby!

While each member of the crew pursued varied academic class schedules, the crew shared in a stream of fun times with Frisbee on the lawn in spring, competitive ping-pong in the winter and attending free musical concerts, (such as Helen Reddy—not very good, Poco, Procol Harum and the James Gang). Long dinners together in the cafeteria were spiced with conversations about many daily pursuits (mostly women) and the keggers at the local gathering spot, an old deserted water filled mining quarry (known only as the Quarry). Keggers were social extravaganzas administered by upper-classmen featuring no ID checks and always featuring the fine (sic) classic, cheap local beers of the Midwest's sky blue waters: Hamm's, Grain Belt and Schlitz; all served in the inimitable plastic ribbed cup for a only $1.

An important series of influences served to coalesce for Mark in the spring of 1971. A crazy combination of friends with cars, music concerts, academics, concussion syndrome and drinking at keggers that fused into a surreal, dreamlike experience that Mark never forgot, but in truth, never truly remembered. *What?!* This episode of Mark's college days was triggered by his love of music. In the spring of '71, the super band, Chicago, was doing a rare Minnesota appearance at the venerable Minneapolis Auditorium and Mark and two friends were going to the concert, driven by Greg in his nice new Pontiac Trans Am.

Being unfamiliar with the big city traffic, the boys had a high-speed collision while running a red light prior to the concert. Everyone was fine, except Mark, who had unknowingly suffered a concussion. Mark immediately developed an intense amnesia, causing aimless and risky wandering in the middle of the busy main street of Hennepin Avenue. An overnight hospitalization for observation was required and triple bummers, the Chicago concert was missed, and Greg's beautiful Trans Am was a wreck.

Mark was released with the stern medical directions that his friend Greg was responsible to arrange for round the clock observation, including waking him up during the night and escorting him to classes until he had re-aligned his altered neural pathways. Jumping forward to the twentieth century, sports medicine mandates a comprehensive concussion evaluation protocol for sports and accidents. But back in '71, if you had a concussion and you could identify the number of fingers and what day it was, you were good to go. During his days as a varsity high-school gymnast, Mark recalled two episodes of concussion that were treated by willful and skillful neglect and resolved without any noticeable sequelae, except perhaps, a twisted sense of humor and a love for the essence of a well designed prank.(More about that later)

As evidence of this twisted sense of humor, Mark's favorite comic magazines vacillated between *Mad* magazine and the *Fabulous, Furry Freak Brothers*, coupled with a true love of the movies; *Animal House, Harold and Maude* (a cult classic with continuous shows in selected Minneapolis theaters for over a year) and years later the ridiculous, raucous *Blind Date* (don't get her drunk, was the sage advice). Learning from mistakes is reputed as evidence of intelligence and in the case of his own future dates (damn few), Mark definitely abided by the *Blind Date* movie advice to avoid getting her drunk.

During this recovery period of his orientation, Mark and his friend, Greg had been warned that he must not drink any alcohol for at least one week. Of course, with the bravado and deep intellect of college young men, Mark decided with the wise counsel of his crew of friends that he was recovered suitably in only three days and therefore, was now sure that the big Friday night kegger was definitely safe to attend. Besides, Mark wasn't going to drink much and local knowledge had determined that two very hot young ladies with no known boyfriends were also attending the very same kegger. How awesome, man!

Well, according to his crew, Mark was having a fabulous time dancing and drinking and bonding with one of the two hot un-escorted ladies (no names will be shared—because they aren't recalled) and when it was time to leave the party in the communal vehicle for that night, Mark nor his date were nowhere to be found .

Although the crew was well lit and the night was dark, they were lucid enough to realize that Mark in his post-concussion condition may have not been in good shape or even possibly in serious physiologic or neurological distress. After thirty minutes of diligent searching the area around the old deserted quarry, the surrounding woods, remaining parked cars and the shore of an adjacent lake, they were unsuccessful in finding Mark and they left with the consensus belief that Mark had taken off with the unnamed lady. Ken announced to the guys, "Let's go, he'll find his way home later."

Sunrise light, the sound of gentle waves against a boat, a wetness against his hand and a swaying motion to his bed were all images meshing in and out of Mark's consciousness as in waking from a deep sleep dream state. Suddenly, Mark jerked more alert, slowing realizing that he was not in a dream. As harsh reality set in, he realized he was sprawled in a small boat with a headache, a sweaty forehead and a poor visual focus. Indeed, he was looking directly ahead at an unknown girl dressed in a red sundress, covered with a sweater and smeared make-up on her contorted face. As she slept, a slight line of drool escaped at the corner of her mouth. *Holy crap, thought Mark, what in the heck is going on here and where am I? Who is this girl?*

Now, with the impact of a jackhammer, Mark recalled

being at the kegger, apparently with this girl and as it appeared, had slept overnight in this boat in the middle of
this lake. *What had they done? What lake is this?* Amid this
flurry of pertinent questions, the surging awareness of the
time hits home. Damn its 7 am,and Mark's schedule seared
through his haze, *I have my psychology final this morning at
8 am !! God, I can't miss that!* A layer of fear, melding with
adrenaline are now powering up Mark's consciousness as he
sits more upright, locates an oar and yells at his boat-mate
(the emphasis on boat, versus mate).

"Hey, you in the red dress, wake up, wake up!" She offers no response and no movement results. Since it is unwise
to stand up in a canoe and go to the front of the canoe and
shake this girl awake, Mark frantically resorts to knocking
the oar against the bottom of the boat and screaming louder.
"Wake it up!" As the drowsy and hung-over young lady
rouses from her sleep, she rubs her reddened eyes, glances at
Mark and smiles ; "Dang, that was quite a night, wasn't it.?"

"I don't really remember" mumbles Mark, embarrassed
both by what he might have done and not even remember-
ing her name, "but we need to get this boat to shore, so
pickup the paddle and starting rowing. Now!" "Oh, no,
I don't feel so good," she replies with a yawn and stretch
of her arms. As we know, without wind, sound carries for
great distances over still water. Mark's frantic screams had
alerted the local farmer on whose property sat the lake and
in whose boat, the rapid rowing Mark and the wiped out
girl in the red dress were seated.

After a few desperate minutes, the sweating, dehydrated
and exhausted and slightly panicked Mark arrives at the
lake shore, to be greeted by the resident property owner /

farmer wearing a red plaid shirt, denim coveralls and a sarcastic half-grin. "Hey bud, did you have a good boat ride last night?" "Ahh, I'm really sorry, man, ah sir, if we took your boat, but I have to get back to campus in a hurry!" Can you give me a ride..., please?"

Chuckling, the farmer gazes at the girl, who is now standing unsteadily, supporting herself next to a tree trunk and smoothing out her dress and her hair. "H'mm, what about her, son?" "Well, I guess she is on her own, but I got to get to campus (current time now 7:28), please can you help me, I 'll pay you" persisted Mark. More chuckles from the farmer as he considers; "Which campus are you headed to anyway and how much do you have?." "Well sir, I need to go to St. Cloud State"Mark fumbles for his sweaty wallet, "I have $7, sir."

"OK now, young man with the unnamed girlfriend, you can see I have a tractor here, and you are a long way from St. Cloud State, but I will take you to the highway (the farmer is referring to US-10) and I will take your girlfriend to the house and she can call who she needs to." "Keep your money, buster, and what's your name, dear" once again looking at the girl and as he starts the tractor. The suddenly loud tractor motor causes Mark's head to start throbbing and the noise masks her tearful response, but he is able to hear the farmer; "He ain't much of a gentlemen, is he?"

The sting of humiliation is now magnified by this desperate predicament. Damn! Now the words to Steppenwolf are ringing in Mark's aching head: Yes, head out on the highway, but not this type of adventure! Well, this must be the "whatever comes our way" part.

After a short ride on the tractor to the highway, Mark

fortunately hitchhikes with a fellow college student who drops him off at campus, only two short blocks from the building where the psychology test is being given. Mark sprints to the building and busts through the door to the classroom as the bell rings and in this case, the outer doors are locked by the graduate assistants. *Wow, am I lucky!* Mark's old friend from high school, Ken, whom he rode with to the kegger is seated two rows in front of him to Mark's right and he turns and mouths "where in heck have you been, you look like crap!"

All Mark can do is smile, wipe the sweat off his forehead with his left sleeve and give the silent thumb-up with his right hand as the graduate student hands out the test document. Needless to say, Mark's prior night and this morning's physical activities were NOT the intended method to prepare for a final test, so Mark was also gripped by a primal fear that his effort would produce a failing grade. Compounded by the nervous butterflies, his stomach was attacked by the gnawing feelings of not having eaten for fifteen hours and the churning after taste of multiple (how many, who knows) cheap beers.

Although psychology is a standard in general studies curricula and is often an unpopular requirement for many college students, this particular psychology was both anything but standard and therefore, was fairly popular among freshmen and sophomore students. The class was taught by a professor who had been a graduate assistant for B.F. Skinner, famed for his operant condition-ing approach to learning. The class was invested in immediate reinforcement for responses to the presented material and both homework and class-work were presented in an interactive style.

The final test answer sheet was a shade the dot document which was fed through an electronic scoring machine immediately after finishing the test. Incorrect responses would register a clicking sound and the student would be handed his final score out of a possible one-hundred in a matter of seconds, while standing in front of the machine, the professor and waiting classmates.

Mark took the entire one hour to take the test, and consequently, was one of the last students in line to suffer the scoring machine torment (ah, rather the immediate feedback). As the answer sheet was passed through the machine, Mark's heartbeat raced and he imagined he heard only a single click, but was unsure. Mark looked at the graduate assistant with doubt, as the graduate assistant took the sheet out and offered," Hey, no problem,we'll just run it again."

As he stood waiting, Mark began to sweat again plagued by wildly rampant thoughts of failure dancing in his head. After the repeat pass-through, the grad assistant glanced at the sheet, handed it to him and exclaimed, "Nice work!" Woo, hoo, what an amazing sight! The scoring machine was right the first time. Existing at the edge of sheer disbelief, Mark was looking at a score of ninety-nine and a certain A for the class! How purely psychological !!!

Thus, Mark may have accidentally set a new trend for test preparation with the following potential formula: suffer a concussion with lingering amnesia, get drunk on an empty stomach the night before, pass out and get little or no sleep, awaken with no breakfast, a churning nausea and a dehydration headache, paddle a boat furiously for ten minutes and sprint full-out for five-hundred yards for a little morning aerobics immediately preceding the test. Do you think it will catch on?

During the first quarter of school as freshmen, this odd fellow appears in an un-recalled way to become a begrudged addition to the crew-Denny Clifton Ridge. Denny hailed from the ritzy Minneapolis suburb of Edina, famed for super competitive and successful high school sports as well as its affluent citizens. No one takes credit for his introduction to the existing members, but after October he became a constant, generally unwelcome and frequently uninvited companion to any social event around the campus.

Unlike the rest of the crew and most other college students, Denny wore expensive cashmere cardigan sweaters and corduroy pants to class, always had short, carefully groomed hair and colored matched leather shoes. While Denny was a nuisance barely tolerated by the other members of the crew, he was particularly irritating to Mark. Denny was a perpetual fifth wheel, three's a crowd hanger-on and would frequently, mysteriously show up when Mark was out on a date or on a concert event. Bummers. Moreover, Denny was not easily dissuaded from interrupting private time, despite gentle requests to bug off, baby.

During a post-meal chat session at the dining hall, Greg, Dan and Ken felt he was just a lonely guy who meant no harm, and advised Mark to just cool it and talk to him once in awhile. *Ok,dudes, I'll give it a good ol' college try*, decided Mark against his best judgment.

Dan turned and announced, "Hey Mark, here he comes now!" "Hey guys, how's it going? I was just over at the library and thought you all might be here, so I'll just join you. What's good tonight?" Dan and Greg simultaneously announced "The pasta shells were great. Yea, we got to get back to studying, so we'll see you later." Turning in their meal trays, they smiled back at Mark as Ken stood and nodded, "Yeah, I got to hit the books too. Later, gents."

Wow, thought Mark, this feels like some sort of set-up for real. "Hey Denny what are you going to major in?" searching for something genuine to say "Well, Mark, I really haven't decided yet, but what would you advise?" "I am not a career counselor, dude!" objected Mark. "What do you want to do after school, anyway?"

Denny hesitated a moment, sighed, then uttered, "My grandpa and my Dad, want me to be an attorney, but I just don't know about that. But Mark, you just seem to know what you are doing. You are on scholarship for English, right?"

"That's right, Denny" replied Mark tersely, desperately considering a graceful, but definite exit line. "Well, maybe, I'll be an English major and then we can take some classes together, right?" *Let me outta here,* thought Mark "That still doesn't answer the question of what you want to do, Denny."

"Well really I think I'd like to design outdoor mazes or labyrinths. Do you know the difference, Mark?" *What the crap does that refer to anyway?* thought Mark darkly. "No, I guess I don't." "Well, a maze is a group of interconnected passages with a definite exit, while a labyrinth has blind dead-end zones that must be back tracked." "Hey, Denny, I don't know where you get this stuff, but I think you should stick with the attorney gig. Have a good one." asserted Mark as he stood to escape and rushed out of the cafeteria.

Several other episodes of Denny's interference and

harassing type behaviors occurred during that fall quarter, with Mark and others in his crew. So, taking a leadership role for the crew, Mark hatched a plan of a prank nature to hopefully discourage Mr. Clifton Ridge from any further social irritation.

During the fall quarter, Mark had taken an advanced, upper-class course in Microbiology after an approval interview with his academic counselor, Claude Bestern. During the course, skills were developed in identifying select bacterium viruses and other cellular materials using microscopic exam skills and staining techniques. It seems that all college students have taken classes that were out of their primary focus areas and this qualified as Mark's venture into the uncertain.

Despite the supposed lack of application to Mark's designated major and being the sole freshman in the class, Mark found the class fun, fairly easy and an absorbing type of problem solving exercise in grim contrast to the future, required courses in calculus, physics or organic chemistry. The final test format required students to sequentially stain and test an unknown, assigned sample and make a definitive determination of the assigned sample. From the moment Mark viewed his final test specimen, he believed he knew the identity and he was correct, earning an A for the course.

During the identification process, Mark recalled that his specific sample, a rod-like structure called Bacillus subtillus, was naturally occurring on multiple surfaces and flourished in moist, dark environments and he was stimulated with his prank idea. Mark was struck with how awesome it would be to streak a few samples of the Bacillus on Denny's bath-tub when he left for the winter holiday break of just over two weeks in duration and see what would happen. Denny was one of a few select students in the Stearns Hall with a private room and private bath.

Mark enlisted the help of an unnamed RA (resident assistant) who had a few negative personal conflicts with Denny to open his room and streaked out a generous sample of Bacillus material on his bath-tub and sink, ran water into the bath-tub, turned up the heat to 80 ° F and locked the door. So, Mark would be witness to how much he had learned in his Micro-biology class.

The two-week break passed and as Mark returned to his dorm, he passed by Denny's room where he was greeted by a slightly foul odor and disturbing, oozing wetness spreading from under the door frame. Wow, this experiment had gone crazy! Later that evening, as Mark was relaxing in his own room (located down the hall from Denny's) he heard a loud disturbance, accompanied by a few loud shrieks and then a set of trampling, running footsteps coming from the direction of the Denny room. As Mark turned the corner to witness the disturbance, he saw Denny standing in the hallway with towels and a look of terror and disbelief, surrounded by several hall-mates, a campus police officer and the previously unnamed RA.

"What going on, Denny?" questioned Mark with a degree of mock concern. "Oh, God, my room is all full of some fungus or something and its nasty smelling." "Let me take a look, man." Mark responded. As he walked into the bathroom he was stricken with a terror flick type scene: the bathtub was fully coated with the most vile, moist and slimy layer of green crap resembling an advancement of the green ooze monster. Well, unfortunately for Denny, the experiment worked beyond Mark's imagination and although there was never any direct accusation from Denny about deliberate biologic terrorism or neighbors responsibility, Denny was subsequently absent from any crew activities for the remainder of the school year. And while no crew members can recall what became of Denny, we might wonder if he became an attorney with a hobby of making mazes.

Part II. DEPARTURE

Two years of college at St. Cloud State passed rapidly, culminating with Mark's departure from the accelerated English track due to a bitter disagreement with the department Chair about the correct composition of an allegory. Mark's resulting assignment to report to a remedial writing lab in order to achieve a passing grade for the class was humiliating. What abject disillusionment, Mark could not become a writer, if he couldn't even finish his English degree! NOW WHAT?

With no future in pursuing English with this particular professor, Mark's plans for the future mutated to another interest: the treatment and management of athletic injuries. Inspired by his own personal frequent need to recover and tolerate varied injuries during his collegiate gymnastic career, Mark became intrigued by the concept of injury healing.

During the early 1970s, two parallel emerging health science professions were directed to the practice of injury management: consequently, athletic training and physical therapy became contending choices for Mark's future professional degree plans. Mark sought out the advice of a local pioneer in the fairly new field of sports medicine As one of very few dually certified Physical Therapist (PT) and Athletic Trainers (ATC), Gordy Graham served as the Head Athletic Trainer at Mankato State College *(now renamed as Minnesota State-Mankato)*. Without equivocation, Gordy recommended that being trained and certified as both a PT and ATC, would offer the greatest career opportunities. Certainly, Mark is indebted to Gordy as one of his first professional mentors.

Regrettably, no programs in sports medicine, athletic training or physical therapy existed at St. Cloud State. Therefore, Mark decided to transfer to the big school an hour to the east, the University of Minnesota in Minneapolis. A transfer to the U of M, predicated a vast change of plane; in course concentration and difficulty, in campus and city magnitude and in the potentially overwhelming loss of personal friendships and identity due to the immense size of the student body. At this moment, while reflecting back on his preteen daydream on the curb long ago, Mark realized it was all clicking into reality: a major big city, an eminent university degree and then, vast opportunities with a professional degree would be in reach.

Located near downtown Minneapolis, one of the largest metro areas in the mid-west, the University of Minnesota is also traditionally one of the largest student body enrollments in the nation (in that era it was common to have an enormous student enrollment of 52,000)[6]. In addition, the

---

[6] University of Minnesota. Office of Institutional Research:2000-2102. Student Enrollment Statistics.

U. of M. offered a respected two year credentialed professional program leading to a B.S. degree in Physical Therapy and this level of preparation appealed to Mark's new focus and commitment to the practice of sports medicine – defined as the prevention, treatment and rehabilitation of sports and recreational injuries. The term *"rehabilitation"* was a new concept introduced into the medical professions in the mid-1970s.

The U. of M. Physical Therapy Program demanded a challenging compilation of human anatomy, bio-science, exercise physiology, communication skills and a vast array of manual techniques that culminated in sitting for a nationally based professional licensing exam. Consequently, Mark learned with some concern that not only was a high grade point average necessary for admission into the program, but the selection process only picked thirty two students for each class which represented only a 10% success ratio of applicants (roughly the same qualification ratio for the vaunted Navy Seal program of later decades). Among prospective health science students like Mark, it was assumed knowledge that getting into PT school at the U of M was more difficult than getting into either medical school or law school – but mercifully carried a whole lot cheaper tuition load.

H'mm, thought Mark, *this sounds like a good challenge and an even better career path.* Mark spent his junior year taking more required preparatory science courses, doing recommended volunteer work in the Children's Rehabilitation Center on campus and working as the well-paid director/coach of a privately owned gymnastics academy.

Due to limited finances, Mark existed in a quasi-bohemian

state of poverty, with minimal food cooked at home, infrequent booze and continued transportation on an old, used bicycle. Nonetheless, Mark was sufficiently fueled by determination and dedication to his new career commitment. During this year the young college student developed what he would mentally summon during all tough times or during daunting tests, as his SSS—self sustaining spirit.

Finally, filled with great joy and celebration, Mark was victorious in being selected for the 1973 physical therapy class, which was historic for accepting the first four male students. Beginning with the inception and progression of the physical profession as rehabilitation nursing in the early 1950s, the profession had developed as a predominately female practice.

With the distinction of a male PT student came a subtle pressure for these guys to achieve success, because as one of the senior professors indelicately maintained that "these guys are an experimental group with a suspect chance of finishing". For Mark's dedication, nothing could beat that type of in-your-face challenge, sort of an educational trash talking that fired up his motivation to finish with the highest grades and to pass the difficult eventual professional license exam. *Rely on the SSS*, reasoned Mark and you will prevail and succeed.

Due to his sacrifice in gaining acceptance to PT school, Mark became focused (perhaps driven is a more accurate term) on mastery of each subject and full immersion in lab projects with the goal to fully grasp the nuance of the situation and to become the most prepared and highly informed professional that he could possibly be. This level of single-minded purpose would often clash with the communal efforts of fellow students or the careful plans of the instructors.

Resembling his long ago fourth grade experiences; Mark was occasionally sent to the principal's office (actually now entitled program director) for attitude remediation. The red haired, bespectacled Mr. Moen was a genteel fellow, but more than a little tired with the distraction of counseling Mark to adopt a more kind and gentle approach to his daily studies and a more respectful interaction with certain, designated faculty members.

Currently, national physical therapy programs take three years leading to a DPT (Doctorate of Physical Therapy), but Mark's program was only two years. Nevertheless, it was still a long, arduous and rewarding two years. Analogous to the Navy SEAL process, each month posed a more difficult academic or practical challenge, engendering their motto;

The only easy day was yesterday.

Granted the PT students were not climbing rope ladders, getting wet and sandy, swimming in 60° water or parachuting with HALO jumps, but they were subjected to eight hour classroom days, prolonged lab sessions, frequent tests and incessant practice of interpersonal skills. The result of this two year relentless preparation was the pursuit of clinical professional excellence and a reverent fascination for the inherent beauty of the human machine: it's anatomic marvels and the efficiency in its movement precision.

Riding the bike for transportation was fun sometimes (spring days with no wind or rain and little traffic on the busy University Ave). But bike riding was downright challenging and /or brutal during cold winter days, on icy roads, or when taking out an unsuspecting date; inspired by the nostalgic visions of the bicycle scene in the classic movie, *Butch Cassidy and the Sundance Kid.* This lighthearted scene features Butch carrying the lovely Etta Place on his handle bars(a skill called bucking).Lacking in forethought, Mark asked a attractive nurse to go out on a date to a downtown club. Lacking both a car and cab fare, he picked her up on his bike, safely bucking her across the St. Anthony bridge into downtown Minneapolis.

Apparently her romantic imagination or her mental soundtrack was not in synch with the song :Raindrops Keep Falling on My Head. When Mark called her for future dates, she was suspiciously always busy washing her hair. Funny, as he recalled, her hair was beautiful and seemed very clean. So much for understanding the thought patterns of ladies, which provided an essential change of plane for all future social interactions.

At other times, the bike was not a suitable transportation mode, rendering walking as the only viable, affordable option. An episode of free dental work at the University dental clinic provided a sanguine example. During the first year in PT school, it became necessary to have his wisdom teeth removed (four as he recalled) but Mark had no dental insurance coverage. Following approval for free care within the student health clinic system, Mark was scheduled for the surgery with the instructions that he could not drive (nor ride a bike) after the procedure.

On a cold winter Friday, Mark was successfully rendered wisdom toothless, issued codeine and released from the clinic. During his two mile walk through the snow covered streets to his apartment building, Mark was still numb from the Novocain and slightly unsteady from the procedure. Consequently, he was repeatedly asked by concerned passers-by if he was OK. Mark's reply was a manly, but slurred "Sss-ure" through his cotton stuffed sutures, despite his unsteady walking pattern and frequent spitting of blood that left an alarming trail into the stark white snow.

The two-year professional PT program surged by, punctuated by ever-changing personal perspectives and newly acquired professional behaviors and a broadening array of therapeutic skills. The delivery of successful patient oriented PT practice requires the raw tools of communication, empathy, belief in exercise and time management. Consequently, the therapist helps the patient achieve their functional goals, or perhaps guides them into realizing more reasonable goals. Mark was a diligent student of these new perspectives.

However to reduce PT practice to merely "helping" people is a flawed misconception. Mark frequently encountered that belief in formal interviews with prospective PT students or during informal advisement discussions with interested young people. Mark was rankled by the hollow statement "that I want to be a PT so I can help people." Mark was forced to choke back an immediate sarcastic response like "well then, become a school crossing guard at a middle school" or a "translator with sign language for the deaf." *Then there would be no need to endure the rigors or the expense of PT school,* reasoned Mark.

The physical therapy educational process is fostered by 3 long-term clinic affiliations in varied settings (for Mark, in outpatient orthopedics, general trauma hospital and a children's specialty hospital), which elicit an end-result of self-confidence and self-awareness. For Mark, this was vividly evident as he viewed and conversed with fellow PT classmates regarding their individual clinical experiences when they returned to campus for continued class-work.

Most stunning of these conversations was the decision-making of Mark's designated lab partner, Rosie. During her first long-term affiliation, she had selected a well-known leprosarium in the South out of interest for working with infectious disease. Her first experience was so gratifying and successful that she was actively recruited by the facility to return for her final internship. At the conclusion of the program, Rosie immediately accepted her first job in that facility and surprisingly (at least to Mark) was promoted to the directorship of the entire facility after some two decades of dedicate employment there.

As a newly licensed and young PT, Mark found it entertaining to field the common patient question, "So, how long have been <u>doing</u> this, anyway?" This rather direct query was usually cached with a tincture of skepticism and mistrust of his professional capability. Most likely, medical professionals in many disciplines also face these slightly irritating challenges to their professional readiness or skills. However, there is a measure of good news lurking behind this issue: as the professional ages and practices longer, this question disappears for awhile. Then, with alarming regularity, the same question may appear again during the third or fourth decade of practice. Now the intent and inflection of the question changes subtly; "Mark, so how <u>long</u> have you been doing this anyway?" No longer is there any implied doubt regarding your competence level, but rather the mildly negative inference about age.

CHAPTER 3.

Sports Time

The fictional Dominican baseball player Chico Escuela(portrayed by so brilliantly by Garrett Morris in Saturday Night Live skits) is famous for the quote "Baseball has been berry, berry good to me!" In later interviews the *real* baseball player, Sammy Sosa repeated the quote, reinforcing it as a reality. However, my favorite baseball quote belongs to the inimitable wit of Yogi Berra who stated in a team meeting, "90 % of baseball is half mental." Huh? It would have been fascinating to be present in that locker room to witness the bemused facial expressions of those players—eager to hear an inspirational or motivational message, but instead receiving a brain twister of guidance. We might call this a mental slight of hand.

Certainly, these quotes are not meant to imply that I am a fan of NY Yankee baseball or more importantly, baseball in general. But Yogi's quote captures the nuances of baseball in some mystical way. You know, the magic of 90 feet between bases and the thrill of four scoreless innings in the so-called pitchers battle. Or how about the pseudo-intensity required to sit in the dugout for three hours, munching on sunflower seeds or spitting chew. Woo, hoo! What excitement!

Now, in truth, baseball is America's pastime. Therefore, it can be argued that it is not a sport. Collectively, we can understand that after 162 games (not including preseason spring exhibition games), the real excitement of the World Series may be caused merely by the exquisite, trembling reality that the season is almost over and now we can truly concentrate on real sports : football, basketball and oh yes, even soccer come to mind.

And so our thoughts digress, but we can now return to an important element of Mark's young life, eventual growth and his evolution. To wit, from the essence of sports rise the changes within him, the recognition of new planes of physical and mental skills. Honestly, sports were also very good to (and for) Mark.

The true intrinsic value of sports may exist within and between several "planes". These planes encompass the development of character and maturity (both physical and mental), learning competition and fair play principles and forging the importance of team concept with respect for authority and discipline.

In addition, time management and timeliness are essential learning points for many young athletes. Yet somehow, time management persists as a difficult challenge even for adult pro athletes across multiple sports. Indeed, we often hear of athletes being fined for missing team meetings, or being late for team practices or travel departures. While some occupations or life phases do not seem to demand time precision, if kick-off time is at 1 pm on Saturday and the athlete arrives at 1:02 he just won't be in the game. It's just that simple, that unequivocal.

While appreciative of the complexity and depth of sports

lessons, Mark also treasured another frequent benefit of high school, college and professional sports. For Mark, the opportunity for free travel for road games was always educational and therefore, enjoyable. While some destinations were exotic or famous (like New York City and San Diego) many others were not so intriguing, but they all served to expand Mark's concept of the great North American landscape. Admittedly; it has been said that no one enjoys a travelogue of pictures from someone else's trip, so we will forego the slide show, but proceed with a series of selected travel adventures instead.

From the aerial viewpoint of the ground while flying in an airplane; new ideas and fresh perspectives freely emerge. The world appears from an elevated perspective and the resulting "change of plane" may be a guiding influence. Objects and people that are large and imposing at ground level, now seem less significant, less concerning or even trivial. Travel by any mode of transportation: walking, running, by kayak, bicycling or by car; all may impact the emotional set of various people, prior places and past events, but they lack the same degree of visual stimulus that is experienced during flight.

Mark's earliest travel experiences revolved around sporting events. Aside from memorable family trips as a youth: the Michigan trip previously described, to Tucson, Arizona during a Christmas break and to the boundary waters of northern Minnesota lake country, sports trips were the dominant travel outlet for young Mark.

Although famous for its high level, high school hockey; the other major Interscholastic sports in Minnesota in the mid- to late 1960's were football baseball, basketball and interestingly a huge presence of gymnastics for men. The burst of interest in women's gymnastics from the Olympics competition, with such sensations as Olga Korbut, had yet to enthrall American athletes, their families and huge audiences.Inspired by Olga's triumphs in 1972, most Olympics Games gymnastic competitions lead in total audience attendance figures, rivaled only by track and field venues.

Mark participated in several sports during junior high. He started with football, but a mere two practices and two games were sufficient to prove to him that physical collisions with other humans was not a desirable recreation. He then moved on to basketball (a personal best of 28 points in a game in which the entire team scored only 48!) and American Legion summer baseball league as a second baseman. None of these sports were magnetic attractions for Mark, who nonetheless enjoyed physical activity, the thrill of competition and the challenge of any physical skill mastery. When faced with physical limitations, Mark soon learned the value of concentration to the details of body mechanics and an understanding of the rules with varied sports.

Mark's initial motivation to play football was quickly squelched, when playing junior high defensive end. He attempted to break up a team sweep play to his side of the line, resulting in an impact to his right forearm which immediately swelled into a hard, thick knot the size of baseball. While scary to look at and painful the coaches were not very concerned or sympathetic about a "little bruise". During that era, athletic trainers were not available to render acute treatment for high school sports.

Respectively; Mark's true character loved the thrill of individual sports, which were not dependent on the play of team-mates, but wholly determined by his own efforts, his heart and his own practice, concentration and skill. Thus, after his independent experimentation with tumbling and self-invented gymnastics moves performed in the municipal park across the street from his home, he became hooked on the proprioceptive feelings of being upside down, flying backward and gradually mastering the control of his own center of gravity, body weight and postures.

At age twelve to thirteen, during warm weather months (and there were damn few in Minnesota), Mark was routinely in the neighboring park performing self-guided and imagined gymnastic tricks, sometimes to admiring audiences of younger neighborhood kids.

His activities were also closely and surreptitiously watched by a neighbor, Bob, from his front picture window. How ironic, it must have seemed to Bob, that a neighbor kid would independently choose to do gymnastics in the park. Because Bob was not only a teacher at the William Budd Junior High School where Mark was a seventh grader but moreover, Coach Bob also served as the junior high gymnastic coach.

Mark's small hometown was notorious for producing a dynasty of successful gymnastic teams. In fact, this small town was amazingly rated by the big city newspapers of Minneapolis as a top-ten gymnastic team on a continuous basis for fifty years!

Naturally, Mark was recruited to participate on the junior high team and excelled at tumbling, trampoline, floor exercise and eventually the side horse. Modern collegiate and Olympic competition in men's gymnastics includes several separate events: floor exercise, rings, side horse, vaulting horse, high bar (a.k.a. horizontal bar) and parallel bars. Whereas In the 1960's,gymnastic competition also included trampoline and tumbling. The costs of a gymnastic program were minimal compared to sports such as football; providing a possible explanation for the wide prevalence of the high school sport in Minnesota at that time.

With swift reversal, the prevalence of scholastic gymnastics was weaned out of competition. During the 1980s, gymnastic's lawsuits and resulting insurance costs spiraled out of control, due to grievous spinal injuries that were most often suffered during participation on the trampoline.

Although, the trampoline served as an excellent teaching tool for many primary gymnastic skills, it also produced a potential risk for uncontrolled falls off the elevated bed to the hard, unyielding floor. Effective injury prevention could be ensured by adequate coaching supervision, skilled spotters and suspended belts and appropriate, adjacent protective mats or specialized crash pads .Sadly, these critical protective elements were lacking throughout American gyms and gradually, painfully, high school gymnastics followed the path of the dinosaurs: extinction due to increasing pressure of exorbitant lawsuits and threats to school districts financial status.

Two breakthrough moments (no pun intended) powered Mark's eventual competitive gymnastic career. In both episodes, an uncontrolled movement caused a high altitude fall resulting in a radial fracture, known in orthopedic terminology as a Colles fracture. This common fracture of the forearm, often in young athletes or from play activities, affects the bone on the thumb side of the lower arm(the radius).The fracture often produces a bony deformity resembling the shape of an inverted fork utensil, which is a graphically disturbing image for the uninitiated lay person.

First of all, in the very same neighborhood park where Mark practiced gymnastics, he also enjoyed swinging on the wooden seat swing set, which supported a standing position. Of course, this type of seat allowed harder and harder efforts in propelling the swing to pump as a high as possible into free space. Common wisdom dictates that it is impossible to actually fly the swing backward over the cross bar of the swing set. But Mark was undeterred in his personal quest to prove basic physics (or maybe common rumor) to be incorrect. Finally, on a calm early fall day, Mark was successful in his energetic final pump and as witnessed by several awestruck local lads, flew the swing unfettered over the cross bar and outward in a gorgeous arc through the clear blue, wind-less sky.

Viewing the ground from above, Mark momentarily sensed a giddy feeling of victory, sheer weightlessness and a floating sense of physical freedom. Then the cruel nature of gravity teamed with momentum and stripped Mark's desperate efforts to grip the swing chain. Mark flew off forward at high speed, falling the twelve feet to earth. Rapidly reaching the ground, Mark made desperate efforts to land on his feet, but overcome by the intense rotational force, his feet snapped past the ground. When Mark reached protectively with his left arm, he suffered the aforementioned Colles fracture. The amazed audience of young local kids was understandably grossed out by the altered angle of Mark's arm as he ran home to get medical attention.

Dictated by the prevailing orthopedic practice in those days, the arm was plaster casted from the hand to just below elbow level for an eight-week healing period. Because this happened right at the start of the gymnastics season, Mark was admonished not to go in the gym. Uh huh, Mark could not stay away from the team and practice, so he quietly sat in the gym to observe.

His observation urgency soon erupted into desire for action, and after Mark ruled out all tumbling activity, rings and bars due to lack of grip, only one apparatus remained possible. The dreaded side horse, or pommel horse, was the only event that the wrist cast position allowed Mark to practice. The side horse is often dreaded due to the practice that is required for the precise hand / wrist positions, but in Mark's case the plaster cast acted as a wonderfully constructed wrist brace. It provided a perfect degree of wrist support for practice.

After the eight-week healing period and the daily two to three hour practice sessions exclusively on the side horse, Mark had attained a proficiency level on this event that was usually achieved only by so-called specialists. On his deeply anticipated re-check visit with the treating orthopedist, the physician was pleased with the bony healing, but very perplexed with the drastic wear and weakening of the cast.

"What have you been doing with this cast, anyway, Mark?" questioned the puzzled, but suspicious Doc. "I just think that maybe the cast got a little wet once in the rain" surmised Mark, skillfully skirting the incriminating truth. "Are we taking it off today?" Mark blurted out the hopeful question. "Yes, but no tumbling for another four weeks, do you understand?" A measure of hope had been dashed instantly by further precaution and restrictions. Dang!!!

The doctor's use of definitive criteria and his certainty for healing readiness were impressive concepts to Mark's learning about injury and treatment methods. In addition, the physician's demeanor served as a powerful model to Mark regarding the desirable attributes when dealing with patients. Without conscious thought, this memory influenced Mark's eventual career decision-making process.

The second critical event in Mark's early gymnastic career also involved a forearm, radial fracture. While attending a varsity gymnastic meet as a spectator in ninth-grade; Mark witnessed an excellent all-round junior year gymnast (Jake) fly off the high bar out of control and fall hard to the floor from an eight foot height. Exactly as Mark instantaneously recalled, Jake protectively reached out and there was a sickening crack sound with the resulting Colles fracture, so painfully familiar to Mark.

Compounded by the initial horror of witnessing this injury, Mark was fascinated by the connection between that type of physical force and the resulting type of injury. Mark vaguely realized yet another building block of his eventual career choice, this memory and awareness was also filed away in his sub-conscious for future retrieval during physical therapy school and his eventual career activities.

While bad for Jake, this injury was great for Mark. Due to the loss of this athlete's participation, the team was now lacking one gymnast to score for several competitive events that counted toward the critical team point total. Because Mark was accomplished on the junior high team in floor exercise his coach, Mr Weech, immediately recommended him to the varsity coach as a replacement for Jake.

News of this decision was delivered to him via an

intercom request for Mark to report to the office of Mr.Wolf (the legendary head gymnastics coach) at the end of his second period. Now, Mark was fully distracted from his class work for twenty minutes of suspense. *What was this about, anyway?* wondered Mark, totally unsuspecting of the situation to come. Mr. Wolf was also a senior high gym teacher and varsity baseball coach, but Mark had no direct contact with him, heightening the suspense.

As Mark entered the coaches office, Mr. Wolf looked up from his desk and as was his famous habit, blinked and pulled on his shirt with his right hand. "Hey, now Mark, take a seat there" gesturing to the formed blue plastic chair next to his desk. "Coach Weech believes you have some talent on floor exercise and horse. Is that true?" Feigning modesty as he swelled with pride at this compliment, Mark replied, "Yes sir, coach I like those events, they are really fun." "Well, you know about Jake's injury and we need a replacement for our team, so you are it. I want you to report to varsity practice this afternoon and I will introduce to our men. Is that okay?" "Oh, gosh, Coach, this is awesome!"

"So you see, this is a big challenge here, we've never had a ninth grader before, but we have no other choice, so take this seriously and don't screw up." Mark gulped with a vestige of fear in his voice, "Yes sir!" "Good, I'll call your Dad with the news. He is a good man you know. Now get back to class."

As Mark walked down the polished marble floors of the school, slightly dizzy with surprise and joy, he felt like doing a spontaneous hand-stand in the middle of the hallway! This was an astonishing and monumental development for Mark, because in the history of his school's gymnastic team, a ninth grader had never qualified for the varsity team. His gymnastic career had begun with a bang and would consume a great deal of time and effort during the next six years of high school and college commitment and competition.

In his final year of gymnastics at the University of Minnesota, Mark's coach was Fred Rothliesberger, a renowned and demanding leader, who had served as the Men's US Olympic Gymnastic Coach. Coach R's rigorous practice schedules were wearing Mark down to the point where he couldn't stay awake to study at night. Due to these school-work time constraints, growing intolerance of sucking it up through varied injuries (fortunately non-disabling or chronic) and dwindling motivation, Mark's career ended with a whimper and he left the University of Minnesota practice squad to concentrate on Physical Therapy School preparation.

Mark was left with the satisfaction of progressing with difficult physical stunts, mastering new skills and the thrill of competition were lasting imprints of memory. In particular, Mark was known for his signature flashy flexibility move in floor exercise, in which he landed from a head-spring into a sudden full front split. (Figure 3.1)

As a young male, classically imbued by perceived immortality and resilient with the musculo-skeletal visco-elasticity of youth, Mark never worried about staying physically fit. The passion for gymnastics had fulfilled that need for many years. But now during the enforced sitting demands of collegiate reading, classroom and studying (of course, before the internet and WiFi); Mark realized new physical pursuits were going to be necessary.

Early during his education, Mark perceived the drawbacks of prolonged sitting. He also yearned for a fun, physical activity and the added challenge of competition. After many evenings of rigorous research in the campus library, Mark would notice the complaining stiffness of his knees and lower back when descending the grand staircase of the library entrance.

Current science now guides us to avoid continuous sitting for more than two hours because it leads to potential heart failure[7], promotes postural strain in the knees and lumbar/cervical spine and is certainly a risk factor for the Americanized propensity for obesity and Type II diabetes[8]. For recreationally active people and competitive athletes, prolonged sitting also fosters hamstring tightness, which predisposes the individual to time-loss hamstring strains. Furthermore, sitting less than three hours per day could add more than two years of life expectancy.[7]

The large majority of human skeletal muscles respond to hard labor, intense weight training and aggressive military or athletic training by becoming leaner, stronger and larger in mass. The most striking exception is the gluteus maximus; with training or physical exertion, the butt actually becomes visually smaller. Hence, the visible dangers of sitting are cosmetically obvious. In fact, as Mark recognized from years of studious observation, the signature shape of an inactive, prolonged seated butt muscle; the dreaded "chair-butt" was not a rounded and firm form, but

[7] Young, DR, Reynolds K, Sidell MA et al. 2015. Abstract P133: Effects of Physical Activity and Sedentary Behaviors on Risk of Heart Failure. American Heart Assn Meetings.

[8] Hellmich,N. 2015. If you want to cut heart failure risk, don't just sit there. USA Today

a squared off and soft look that has gradually assumed the imprinted shape of the preferred chair seat that the owner frequents.

A daily dose of bike riding for transportation alone did not fill the bill for Mark. *What should I select?* questioned Mark, considering time constraints, access and expense factors. Thinking poetically, Mark foreshadowed his future commitment with exercise:

> Ashes to ashes
> Dust to dust
> Meanwhile, move we must
> Or we shall surely rust!

Racking heavy weights in a gym did not appeal to Mark and he was absolutely uninspired by the rat on a flywheel nature of running on a treadmill. Inspired by the physical and emotional intensity of the great, late night college rec.-room table tennis tournaments, Mark gravitated toward racquet sports for exercise and fun.

During Mark's first year in PT school, he reconnected with Jerry, his old friend from the gymnastic team at St.Cloud. Jerry was now married and employed at the eminent and beautiful complex of the Edina, Minnesota YMCA. This facility offered many fine athletic activities including a series of gleaming, white racquetball courts and Jerry and Mark began to play undisturbed for long sessions after normal member hours.

Racquetball play was sheer excellence! Mark and Jerry loved the fun, fast and furious pace of the game, the sweat-drenching competition and the full-out smashing of the defenseless little blue ball. For Mark, it also offered a welcome tension release from the ardor and discipline of acquiring his new professional credentials and persona as a physical therapist.

Mark also reveled in the echo chamber effect created by emotive screaming, yelling and guttural grunts during the game The glass and cement box also reverberated with periodic screams of pain when the high-speed ball would bury itself deep in the tissue of the lumbar or calf areas, twisting a deep achy bruise.

As any racquetball player knows, when caught standing between the back wall and the opponent's intended line to the front wall, it is a perfect invitation to stripe the ball into your opponent. Play is stopped when the back player calls what is termed "a hinder", and the point is replayed. However, the advantage is now clearly for the "hindered" player, as the wounded opponent temporarily limps around the court. The hindered player is also afforded a strategic advantage, when the wounded player is hesitant to jump in front of their opponent again.

After several years of pick-up and league racquetball competition, Mark won a weekend racquetball tournament, winning a pair of Lotto shoes and the chance-of-a-lifetime opportunity to play a fund-raising promotion against none other than the famed world champion player of the era, Marty Hogan. This opportunity proved to be a dubious honor, however. To the small, vocal crowd observing in the glass walled exhibition court, Mark put up a good fight, actually winning the first point and momentarily leading 1-0.

Pumped by the adrenaline from the crowd's applause, Mark was ready to deliver the same corner-pinched, lob serve to Marty's backhand. When Mark turned to see if he ready, he was startled to feel a soft tap on his back with Marty's racket with the threatening words delivered in a quiet voice, "Nice serve, man, but you won't get that in again!" Accepting the competitive challenge, Mark proceeded with the same exact serve and true to his word, Marty effortlessly took the point because he was actually standing sideways in the target corner, to easily scrape the serve away with an explosive slam. And now the rout was mercilessly on: final score —World Professional Champion 21, weekend tournament champion 1.

For Mark, it was a fun and wholly humbling experience. He had never witnessed the speed and power of Marty's play and runs and he was absolutely stunned to see him actually dive head-long to retrieve Mark's lowest, hardest front wall "kill" shots. During his normal matches, those very same kill shots were automatic, walk away and grin, winners.

Post-match, Marty graciously attended a photo session for club members, and at the conclusion, Marty approached the smiling, but exhausted Mark; "Hey, bud, don't take it too hard. Most of my pro tournaments opponents never even score a point." commiserated Marty. "Well, thanks for being here. You are incredible, and I learned a lot today." answered Mark.

Later on during his year and a half residence in Hollywood, Florida, Mark joined a highly popular racquetball league, and applying some of the lessons from his crushing exhibition match, actually won the annual class B club championship with a large trophy as the winning prize.

Gradually as the years passed, the forward bending and lunging move-ments required in racquetball, began to increasingly irritate Mark's lower back. Plagued by a chronic lumbar condition, Mark would suffer stiffness and pain during basic daily activities for a few days following a match and Mark regretfully realized, that once again, it was time to acquire a new fitness activity. While the trophy is still on display, the truest joy was the intrinsic reward of fighting though his own fatigue and the intensity of his respected opponent to slide into victory (and later collapse on the hall floor bathed in sweat).

As humans we are all physical animals; trapped by an innate need to move, an ingrained ability to run as the remnant of our prehistoric "fight or flight" response. As a varsity gymnast and golfer, Mark was never dependent on running skills. Therefore, running as an exercise was not a familiar basic skill and was definitely <u>not</u> a true passion. But things changed as gymnastics and racquetball were eliminated by evolutionary ruling out. Or maybe it was the wimpy surrender to physical aging and career rationalization. But in any case, a new plane of exercise was becoming both necessary and imminent.

During the start of the fitness craze, the running popularity boom surged to public awareness in the early 1970's. Motivated to find a new physical pursuit, Mark joined the legions of citizen-runners (so termed by Alberto Salazar)[9] Mark considered his initial efforts as merely a trial to select a readily accessible fitness alternative. He was certainly not harboring any illusions of becoming a running athlete. While gymnastics requires short burst, intense anaerobic runs to produce maximal explosive energy for the vaulting and for difficult diagonal tumbling sequences during floor

---

[9] Salazar, A. & Brant, J. 2012. <u>14 Minutes.</u> Rodale, NY,NY.

exercises; running was not the central focus of training time or practice.

As the "Just Do It"™ culture of activity and sport, fostered by the fledgling Nike shoe company gathered mainstream momentum, Mark joined in and proudly purchased his first pair of specialized running shoes. Mark would lace up the legendary royal blue and yellow swoosh Nike waffle trainers and hit the road in search of fitness, a meditative flow or at least an improvement in pace or achieving distance. As with all novice runners, Mark began to appreciate the aspects of mileage and speed as variables of training changes and began to read Dr. George Sheehan's authoritative works and the helpful articles in Runner's World. Mark made steady progress in physiologic changes and surprisingly, he developed a true enjoyment of the after-effects of running on mood and energy; boosted by all the endorphins, enkephalins or assorted blood sugars that he was supposedly liberating.

Running marked a truly amazing conversion for Mark. No longer just an ancillary training drudgery for gymnastics, Mark was becoming psychologically addicted to the after-effects of running and would adopt this as a lifelong commitment for both fitness and recreational needs. As a running enthusiast (Note: this term is in sharp contrast to skilled running athlete) Mark began to sign-up for various 10K races in the South and as a emerging personal goal completed the famed, massive, Fourth of July party run, known as the Peachtree Road Race. (Fig 3.2)While he received no trophies for this accomplishment, he did get the coveted, legendary emblem T-shirt which cloaked a deep sense of personal satisfaction Once again, like the earlier racquetball victory, at the finish line Mark collapsed in a pile of sweat from the heat and humidity of an Atlanta summer day, potentiated by the proximity of 40,000 fellow sweating runners and fans. No apples or beer at the finish line for him though, a shower and nap would be the trick on this momentous day.

During this era of Mark's career, his private practice physical therapy clinic had employed some fine clinicians who also ran, but at a younger, much more aggressive pace than him. After going on several casual runs with the employees, Mark realized their true talents and proposed that they run as a team in a corporate challenge format. Subsequently, they entered a 10K race with a four person total time corporate competition, completed outstanding individual efforts and amazingly, finished in second place. This time, Mark's team won a huge golden trophy at the podium presentation. Looking down at the collected running teams, Mark's team members were stricken with certain sense of amazement. They had actually beaten the team from Bell South and finished second only to the Coca-Cola ™ team juggernaut: both teams being highly organized and subsidized by their companies.

As a result of Mark's running participation, people would often pose the stereotypical and skeptical question; "God, isn't that running bad for your knees?" As a long-standing sports medicine specialist; Mark will attest to the inherent dangers of running with poorly fitted shoes, lack of lower body flexibility, poor lower extremity postures, faulty mechanics or simple overtraining, but the pure activity of running poses no obvious risk to the knees. In fact, during Mark's thirties and forties, his knees actually did hurt if he didn't run at least every three days! Perhaps then the real question should be, "Isn't not running bad for your knees?"

Interestingly, people rarely ever frame the equivalent question condemning other more high profile sports. For example; "Isn't playing basketball hard on your hands with all those ball impacts?" or "Aren't those football impacts bad for your neck?" And perhaps most obvious, "Isn't that heavy weight lifting hard on your low back?" The answer to the last question is a definite, "<u>No</u>"! While advanced, competitive power lifters hoist massive weights in training and competitions, they rarely suffer from the common, disabling discal injuries that are routinely encountered by many less aggressive or sedentary folks.

The power of correct technique is demonstrated by the power lifters. However, despite the protection of correct techniques; injuries remain an integral, but unfortunate part of competitive athletics. We read many stories of intense human achievements powered by the deep mental concentration efforts in dire circumstances. While the unleashed mind may supersede apparent physical limits, the physical apparatus may become injured by that supreme effort.

Mark's most blazing example occurred during his time working with the XXVI Olympiad in Atlanta, GA. in 1996; notable as the Centennial Olympics. Mark considered himself very fortunate to be appointed to serve as one of the floor sports medicine coverage staff for the Gymnastic Venue, serving both the men's and women's competitions. While the Chinese women's team were the favorites to win the Gold Medal, many experts believed that the US team was also very talented and had a chance to take the Gold Medal with superlative performances.

Although each of the seven member team represented the pinnacle of gymnastic commitment and talent, the star of the team was a diminutive, but powerful, young lady by the name of Kerri Strug. (Fig. 3.3) As the preliminary rounds progressed, the American team was in close competition for the team Gold. Both the media and the fans were intrigued and excited by this development. During the team finals, the American team was only a fraction of a full point behind the Chinese and the entire ladies competition had come to their final rotation, the vault, which was a strong event for the United States (US).

Being the final contestant for the US ladies, Kerri Strug's score was instrumental in winning the team medal. Agonizingly, her score would have to be a perfect ten to win the Gold. And now she was saluting the judges and began her furious run to the vault. As she landed on the crash pad, she twisted her ankle awkwardly; staying down on the mat, in obvious pain, then arose and limped along the runway to confer with her coach about her readiness for the required second attempt. As the floor athletic trainer, Mark was positioned adjacent to the team bench as an estimated two hundred million fans watched live television worldwide.

The suspense of the injury had set a hush on the crowd, concerned for her health and wondering if she even could complete another vault. Both the team physician and Mark attempted to speak to Kerri about the severity of her injury, but were carefully sheltered away by her coach who was fortifying her courage while demanding the absolute necessity for her to not only perform the vault, but to also "stick" the dismount. Failure to stick the dismount would cause the US Team to win only the silver medal instead of the coveted gold. The intense pressure of the moment for Kerri was compounded by her pain and understandable mistrust of her capacity to run at full speed and then land with her injured ankle. Gymnastics is a unique sport in many ways, and if a team-mate or coach implores you to "Stick it!" it is not an insult, but a supportive cheer-up for the gymnast's routine. While gymnastics is performed on an intensely individual basis, it also operates on a pressured, cumulative team basis as well.

Following a short timed break for Kerri's recovery and coaching discussion; she bravely and valiantly stood at the end of the runway and saluting the judges, began her famed and historic run to the vaulting horse. Kerri flew through the air with the perfect height, rotation and flight distance from the horse, breathlessly landed on the crash pad with the slightest knee flexion and then, gloriously mustered a fully erect, controlled and triumphant posture. She then dramatically collapsed on the crash pad, fully consumed by the pain of her ankle and the sheer explosion of emotion from her concerted effort to succeed.

The pride of her mental focus to overcome the pain and channel the pressure of that moment glowed on her face. And oh yes, with the roar of the crowd, came the unbelievable score—a perfect "ten" was flashed on the score boards. The US had won the Team Gold, and little Kerri Strug was wildly and triumphantly carried around the arena by her jubilant and partially crazed coach, Bela Karolyi.

For Mark, that joyful moment was overshadowed by irritation that he was unable to forge through the crazed crowd and photographers, to evaluate and administer initial care for the ankle injury. Contrary to what the media canonized as the athlete who suffered an ankle fracture yet still competed and won; Kerri had actually suffered a moderate degree ankle sprain that was not disabling from subsequent competitions after the Olympics.

Recalling the heady events surrounding Keri's injury, Mark realized that he had witnessed at close range and participated in the care for, arguably the most famous and dramatic sports injury in history. Nevertheless, it remains a statistically certainty that Mark did provide floor coverage during a session for the biggest crowd to ever attend a gymnastic *practice*. Due to a free preliminary practice session held in the huge Georgia Dome an estimated 60,000 fans were in the stands for that fateful day.

Stepping back in time and viewing these pictures on the virtual wall of his memory, Mark realizes the good fortune that his career provided. Indeed, reflecting back on sporting events such as these provided many fertile viewpoints for his ongoing personal and professional change of plane.

CHAPTER 4.

Making a Living

Minneapolis, on the banks of the Mississippi River.

Mark's 1975 graduating class from the University of Minnesota Physical Program decided to opt out of the mass graduation ceremonies on campus and fund a private dinner with their invited families, followed by a class awards ceremony and culminating in the awarding of their diplomas. Instead of restrictive caps and gowns and endless waiting times; the graduates, their families and faculty members enjoyed a quiet, scenic evening on a moored river boat.

Following the diploma presentation, normally quiet Shorty, standing out of the earshot of other parents glowing with pride and several fellow freshly minted Physical Therapists/classmates, offered the concise words of advice which held more challenge than promise ;"Well Mark, the fun is over, now it's time to make a living." *True enough,* thought Mark, amused by his father's cold, practical logic. *Yup, time to get a position that will utilize all the intense training and study of the past four years. Time to venture out into the professional world and make some bucks, develop contacts, open opportunities and I believe, enjoy many interesting and amazing interactions with people and athletes and just like in college, develop some new, and hopefully lasting, friendships.*

"Yea, Dad, I'm already talking to two different places about their jobs and I will keep looking for other interviews. The school here has a great reputation for our students being placed when we finish and I know it won't be long before I land something good."

Shorty grinned slyly. He was probably having suspect flashbacks to Mark's early teen work experience. During summer vacations, Mark's Dad would periodically request help in the family plumbing/HVAC business. Mark's response was routinely punctuated with quiet grumbling and when Shorty required immediate assistance for lifts or supports of materials, Mark's posture caused an all too frequent "hands in the pocket" delay.

"Well good luck with the job hunt, your Mom and I are pulling for you!" "And make sure to let us know, when you do find something." delivered through those pursed lips, evident when Shorty was very serious or angry about a topic. Or was his Dad a little emotional on this special day? "Sure I will, Dad, what did you think of our banquet food?" offered Mark, attempting a quick and not so slick change of topic. "It was alright, but you know I am not fond of damn green beans." came his reply, with that familiar, tight-lipped wry smile.

For Mark, now was the time to start making some money to invest because as the local banker, Byron (a fellow Methodist) always admonished, " You have to realize that retirement is really just around the corner." Well, all that may be true in some unimagined future, but for now Mark had barely started down the proverbial block. As the

Chinese proverb proclaims, *the longest journey begins with a single step.* Now at this juncture, Mark had merely taken step one!

With his previous jobs (lawn-mowing, manual corn de-tasseling, grading crops in a factory microbiology lab), the pay was important but the real thrill had always been learning new skills and any new lessons that emerged from personal interactions. These lessons included how to fake being excited to report to work at 4:30 AM with his supervisors, how to stay awake and function near the end of the night shift (Mark called it the dead-zone of the day at 5 AM, when even birds were silent and even the most hard-core partiers were finally asleep). Mark also learned about the various motivations, hang-ups and rationalizations of selected co-workers with their varied educational levels.

Of utmost fascination was the factory co-worker who worked "on the line" a mind-numbing, noisy, wet environment which required manual placement of fresh corn ears into dangerous cutting mechanisms mounted next to a conveyor belt. Although most of these workers were part-time or seasonal, this particular guy was both a union and a year-round employee. He always took his thirty minute dinner breaks at the same picnic table in the dimly lit designated lunch room. This man always sat alone, made no eye contact and based on Mark's casual but repeated observation, never spoke to anyone.

After two years of summer work which included observing this fellow's daily behavior; Mark's curiosity finally overwhelmed his restraint and he decided to sit down near this man, to make contact and maybe, just maybe find out what was going on with this mysterious man.

"Hey, man, my name's Mark, is it OK for me to sit with you?" "Suit yourself. I know you're a curious kid, aren't you? I've seen you watching me for years now." Well, Mark was just a little surprised by this comment and found himself searching for the appropriate response to this subtly challenging tone of voice. A voice that was neither mean nor friendly, but just intense. "Well, yeah, I guess you get a little curious when you're a student. I work down in the lab and I've seen you on the line."

"No shit, I've seen you around with your fancy white lab jacket and I know who you are. Your Mom is Donna, right, and you are a scab (referring to Mark's non-union status) college kid just here until September 1st to make some money and then get the crap out of here." *H'mmm thought Mark, pretty damn direct, this guy and yet well spoken.* Feeling just a little perplexed by this outpouring of information, Mark ventured on, "Well, sir, I guess you know a lot about me. How do you know my Mom?" "You might remember, that she worked on the line for a few summers also and just like you, she was always trying to talk to me .She told me about you and your college stuff." *Uh-huh, that would be just like my mom.* nodded Mark in silent agreement.

"What about you, I heard that you were a doctor." Laughing loudly with disdain, this man, dressed in a stained smock, waterproof galoshes, a white plastic hard-hat with the factory logo and pair of worn looking safety goggles hanging around his neck, gestured dramatically to himself and exclaimed with mock anger, "Son, do I look like a *Doctor* to you?"

"I guess not." sighed Mark, slightly embarrassed and

becoming unsure of this conversation's direction, questioning whether the decision to talk to this man was very advised. "Well, I'll tell you something, I appreciate your bravery in coming over to say hi and introduce yourself. And yes, you heard right, I *was* a doctor many years ago in Ohio. Like yourself, I worked nights while I was in college at Harvard. "Wow, so what happened?" Mark blurted this out, immediately regretting that he may well have offended this unusual man.

"Well, back then I was a very successful psychiatrist and over time I simply got totally tired of listening and talking about problems. So now I like the steady drone and motion of the line with no conversation. Now you know, and you can keep this all to yourself. And when you see me in the lunchroom in the future, just give me a wave, keep on walking and let me eat my lunch in peace. OK." "OK" agreed Mark as he quickly rose from the picnic table seat, more than ready to retreat. Half-standing, half-crouching Mark hesitated with a key afterthought, "but can tell me your name, sir?" "It's Ruston, now head out."

Impressed by this extreme learning moment with Ruston, Mark realized that physical appearances could be highly misleading and that people react to varied stimuli in vastly personal ways. Serving as in indelible lesson for Mark, this interaction germinated a personal motto that he would adopt later in his career.

The pace of learning associated with each new job opportunity continued. After graduation, Mark's usual good fortune took a brief holiday as he was unable to find a physical therapy job that fit his preferred criteria (collegiate or pro sports medicine position); finally settling for a position in a setting that he had no desire to be in as a contractor to set-up and staff in-house physical therapy departments within nursing homes.

Despite being in what he considered undesirable work setting filled with many depressing patient cases, Mark's first professional job offered an excellent salary, magnified by an attractive performance bonus. In addition, the opportunity to work without direct supervision forced Mark to learn by making independent decisions on patient care, staff training and development and to effectively budget for equipment and staff costs.

Because this job had nothing to do with the sports medicine skills he desired, Mark supplemented his time with volunteer work in covering athletic events in the role of an athletic trainer for Macalester College. Macalester College competed in Division III football, which was not the high level competition bolstered by a huge fan base or packed stadiums. Rather, Macalester was esteemed for an intellectually challenging curricula and a commitment to teaching excellence, comparable to any Ivy League school's mission statement.

Macalester College's promotion literature stressed that their education was designed to provide a "life-altering, life-changing experience with the start of lifelong friendships". Perhaps in naïve fashion, Mark believed this statement represented the essence of every college education, no matter what the school's reputation indicated. Right? However, nothing in this statement emphasizes athletic excellence, the development of professional or Olympic-caliber athletes, nor filling stadiums for monetary income.

As in all human endeavor, sports present ecstatic highs

and degrading lows, sometimes due to bad luck, but more often from poor planning or unwise decision-making. The two years of volunteer athletic training coverage with Macalester was an intense, bittersweet learning experience. Mark was forced to cope with abject, hopeless losing at a level that he had never experienced at any personal level. During his high school tenure, the football team never lost a regular season game, the baseball and basketball teams had winning records and advanced to regional play and his gymnastic team was dynastic in its success. Furthermore, the University of Minnesota football and basketball teams were perennial winners and the Minnesota Vikings of the era were a dominant force.

During Mark's coverage of athletic training; the hapless Macalester Scots football team suffered through the longest college football losing record at any level across the United States. They lost fifty consecutive games, mostly by ghastly margins!! When sports teams in various pregame rituals circle around each and chant some phrase to pump up the team, it is filled with high volume, muscle twitching conviction: go, fight, win. Not so with Macalester's doomed football team. They quietly gathered with a more somber chant resembling a prayer-like hum; "Go, guys, let's not get hurt!"

But they certainly did get hurt, with startling regularity. Injuries to the lineup were a primary cause of losing, even more than the caliber of the devoted athletes desperately supporting each other to win a game, or at least score a few touchdowns or stop the opponent from steamrolling the score. Despite the somber atmosphere of game day humiliations, Mark was immersed in an extensive learning environment about injury management in working with this team. He also sensed the impact of maintaining an upbeat, positive attitude while surrounded by absolute competitive futility, but struggled with his own personal discipline.

Seemingly, losing acts as it's own stand alone injury to the psyche, to the mood and to the competitive spirit. And moreover, losing filters into all other athlete's body parts, like water seeping into a leaky basement. Perpetual losing magnifies the pain of injuries, delays normal healing time and causes annoying recurrences in even easy sports participation. Furthermore, losing in a team context produces greater time loss with injury; whether it is a cause or effect is worthy of further study and discussion. Mark maintains that it is both a cause and an effect.

During the non-winter months, Mark often relaxed during his lunch breaks by walking or just sitting on benches on the banks of the beautiful, iridescent and sylvan setting of Lake of the Isles. This placid in-town narrow lake is surrounded by a paved walking/cycling path and when looking across to the near-by opposite shore, the water appears to be crowned at a slightly higher level than the shore – truly a visual spectacle that can be scientifically termed a meniscus.

For fans who recall the Mary Tyler Moore show, this is where she twirled and smiling, threw her cap into the air during the introductory music. In addition, it is reputed that the famed author H.D. Thoreau often hiked around this and the neighboring Lake Calhoun in the 1860's. Then it can easily be envisioned that the soft fall sunlight glinting off these lakes, could have been the inspiration for the piece

<u>On Golden Pond</u>. Irrespective of this area's past history; Mark found that quiet moments here provided an instant shot of solace from the stressors and the unease of Mark's first professional job.

The nursing home job would have been much less tolerable had it not been for the multiple single, friendly, welcoming and attractive female nurses staffing the various nursing homes under Mark's contract. Whereas visiting physicians would usually produce more work for the nursing staff, Mark's services would generally reduce their workload, by providing physical assists with patients or increasing the patient's physical skills so they were easier to manage in daily tasks.

A year later, the learning continued in a new, desirable dimension as Mark landed his next position as the Head Athletic Trainer for Lincoln University a Division II school located in Jefferson City, the under-recognized capitol of Missouri. Founded as a historically African-American school, Lincoln University had never had an athletic trainer for their sports teams. The new Head Football Coach for Lincoln had just been hired from the Macalester College team and he actively recruited Mark to follow him as his dependable, professional Athletic Trainer (hereafter ATC).

In addition to supplying and organizing the field house athletic training room, recruiting and orienting a local internal medicine physician to serve as the team physician, Mark was further challenged to establish a level of trust among the coaches and athletes, all of whom were black, with minimal if any experience in relating to the role of ATC.

Supplementing the wonderful new travel experiences with the teams to away towns like Cape Girardeau, Missouri,

Dayton Ohio and Itta Bina, Mississippi ; Mark began to recognize the dangers of over-confidence. Although Mark believed his knowledge of anatomy and injury management from PT school and his ATC internships would serve him well; he frequently faced difficult types of emergency situations; i.e., the dreaded face down,unconscious football players after huge kick-off collisions, vexing infection problems with team uniforms, such as impetigo and communicating with an inexperienced and poorly compensated team physician (season tickets to football and basketball and a few paying visits from injured or ill athletes at his office were his reward).

But as this school year progressed, Mark gained invaluable experiences from a series of tests (both in injury care and recognition of behavioral issues) that would always guide his future work. He also gained the reputation with the coaches and athletes—both male and female, that he would provide accurate, concerned and effective care when called upon.

Consequently, he gradually grew as a respected member of the coaching staff, more than a buddy with the athletes. Being just twenty-five years old, Mark was barely older than some of the athletes, when compared to the coaches average ages. In a way, this gradual, steady progression of skills and respect, paralleled the pathway that the vaunted Navy Seal warriors follow, which they eloquently call "evolutions."(More about that later.)

When the school year ended, Mark was called to a meeting with the Athletic Director fully expecting and hoping to receive a much deserved salary and supply budget increase. The tone of the meeting was praiseworthy for

Mark's performance and the newly recognized value of the ATC (athletic trainer) to the sports teams at Lincoln University.

Mark's pulse quickened in anticipation of the next aspect: the bottom line. The Athletic Director began the meeting by commending Mark, "We have really appreciated your contribution and both the football and basketball coaches have come to rely on your expertise and hard work." (While the football program was in a rebuilding stage, the basketball program was historically a perennially winning program with a very established head coach.)

"Unfortunately, your position has lost funding for next season. In view of that,we would certainly like you stay on with us and we'll see if we can get you more money for your supplies." Not being trained in business and the art of negotiation, Mark contemplated the meaning of this situation for the briefest moment, hesitating to formulate the most assertive, yet respectful response, "Ah, are you saying here that I should volunteer for this position?" "Yes, that's pretty much what has developed here." replied the Athletic Director, nodding a silent affirmative response. With a sly chuckle, Mark replied "I'll have to look for other actual work then, but it's been real." *What the crap,* thought Mark, *does this dude take for some kind of idiot? Wow, what an inconceivable insult to my intelligence!*

Following a couple of conciliatory beers (maybe it was more), Mark recognized another emerging change of plane from his first two employment settings: he realized that a stimulating, enjoyable work atmosphere (such as what had developed at Lincoln University),a satisfactory salary level and job security were not always mutually attainable. In addition, it was painfully clear that a suitable salary level was not necessarily commensurate with job satisfaction. NO time for regrets, baby, let's move on to new heights.

As Mark faced new career and interpersonal tests, he recalled his Dad's sparse, but treasured advice about the workplace: "dedicate yourself, work hard and the money will come." *So, when will the money come?* mused Mark, dejected for the moment.

For the first time in six years, Mark was unemployed like many other folks in their post-collegiate mid-twenties; forced to migrate back to his small home town to ignominiously "camp out" in his old bedroom, replete with the same old, small formica desk and nicely crafted set of built-in drawers. Damn, this was not a part of his grand scheme, the vision of his future that appeared on the curb many years ago. As it has been said, people seldom plan to fail, they simply fail to plan.

Yup, Mark guessed that he was now among the humbled and the lost. Then his brain flashed with a sudden flood of his self-worth. *Wait a dang minute, this was Minnesota after all, and self-pity was neither valued nor acceptable in this proud household. And I can't forget, I still am one of the few dually certified Physical Therapists/ Athletic Trainers in the whole country!*

After spending numerous hours in researching and addressing countless letters of application in hopes of securing an ATC job before the start of summer football two-a-day sessions, Mark became more frantic by the lack of response (either by phone or mail, as email was not yet invented) as the summer passed into July. Was he going to end-up working at the canning factory sitting in the lunch room with

Ruston(but not talking, of course)? Despite the occasional spike of self-doubt, his career goal was loud and insistently clear: land a sports medicine position at a major college in a big city and preferably in a warm environment.

And then finally, in a divine moment, that lime green rotary phone in his Mom's kitchen did ring, and his Mom answered politely. "Oh,yesss sir, he is home. I'll get him to the phone, please hold!" With excitement in her voice, Mark's Mom yelled to him in his upstairs room;

"Mark, it's a man from Georgia Tech, who wants to talk to you, he's holding, so get down here quick!" Mark's head was spinning with excitement as he bounded down the stairwell, breathing a little too hard as he picked up the phone, "Hello, this is Mark!" he said, just slightly too loudly and too eagerly. The deep southern voice penetrated the phone receiver (connected to an old school rotary dialed land-line phone), "This is Bill from Georgia Tech. I'm the Head Athletic Trainer here and I received your resume and we have some interest in speaking to you about our position. Would you be willing to come for an interview?"

Talk about the essence of rhetorical questions! "OH, YES Sir, I would!" *Now where was that Georgia Tech located again,* thought Mark as he mentally reviewed his legions of application letters, *Ah yesss, recalling that it was in Atlanta.* "Good, as you may know, the football season is fast upon us and we have some urgency on this matter. I believe that Minneapolis is the major airport nearest to you. Is that right?" "Yes, that's right, sir." "Can you come down tomorrow?" came the surprising question.

The question was like music to Mark's ears, no, maybe more like a symphony. "Ah, yes, yes I sure can." replied

Mark, reeling with surprise at the suddenness of this situation. "Great, we'll have a ticket for you at the Eastern Airlines desk (the now defunct airline carrier was still going strong in those days). Be there by 9 AM, the flight leaves at 10:20 and you will return by 6:20 PM. Alright, now do you have any questions?"

Being too stunned now to think clearly, all Mark could muster was "What should I bring?" *God, how stupid sounding was that,* thought Mark. "Just bring an ID for the flight, and we'll take care of the rest from our end. So, I look forward to meeting with you tomorrow. I will meet you at your gate with your name on a sign." "Thank you so much, Sir. I'll be there! Have a good day." Mark said as he hung up the phone in a state of near rapture.

"What did he say?" questioned Mark's Mom with nervous interest. "I have an interview for the job at Georgia Tech in Atlanta!!" blurted Mark with pride. "Oh, Mark, that is wonderful! When is it?" "Tomorrow!" "Well, how can that be, Mark?" questioned his Mom, with obvious confusion. "They're flying me down there from Minneapolis in the morning!." Coupled with the excitement of a potential job at a great football school in a major city, Mark was going on his first of many plane trips. "Just wait until Dad hears this," exclaimed his Mom, smiling with apparent relief. Mark's thoughts quickly drifted to a key concern, *Maybe this is when the money comes!*

Following the whirlwind of early morning car travel and the plane flight, the next day was filled with meetings with coaches, current athletes and the athletic training staff. Mark's interview process culminated with a private meeting with the Athletic Director in his elegant, upstairs, wood paneled office. As he sat in this prestigious setting, Mark's memories of the long-past interview with Bud Grant, flooded into awareness. *Pay attention, focus and put your feet on the floor!* Mark thought as he remembered the advice his high school Athletic Director had offered prior to the Bud Grant interview.

"Bill, tells me you have some good experience in athletic training, is that right?" came the first question from the AD. "Yes, at Macalester College in St. Paul and at Lincoln University I was the Head Athletic Trainer." "That's good. Here at Tech, we have many sports and additionally, Bill takes care of our travel arrangements. As you can imagine, that's a lot of work. As our assistant trainer here, we will ask that you also do some supply purchasing for things like tape, bandages and some equipment. Does that sound like something you can do?" "Absolutely sir, I've done that with my two prior positions and have always come under the allowed budget."

"Excellent, responded the AD, with apparent approval, "it was nice to meet you and Bill is downstairs, waiting to take you back to the airport." *Wow, that was pretty fast.* mused Mark as he returned to the training room office.

As two men drove back to the airport, Mark was thinking that the interview process was both extensive and had gone well, but he began to fret why no offer had been discussed. Mustering the courage to avoid sounding over-eager, or even worse, desperate, Mark asked Bill, "Do you think I have a chance to get this job?" Met with a direct gaze from Bill and a squinting of his brow, "Yes, you have the job, Mark. We need to have you get back down here, next week." said Bill.

Mark felt instantly exhilarated yet confused, *Why didn't*

I know was hired and what was my salary going to be? As the men parted ways at the airport, Bill handed Mark a sealed envelope with the instructions, "All the position details are reviewed in this letter. Now, if you have questions, you will call the listed number for our human resources person. Welcome aboard. To help you get settled, we have arranged for an apartment for you to live in, at just $100 per month rent, and its really close to campus." *Wow, these guys move fast.* thought Mark as he prepared to board the plane. *I guess this is what it's like to be in Division I, big time athletics!*

Exploding with joy, Mark arrived in Atlanta the next week and was immediately propelled into a whirlwind of change, orientation and adaptation. The first challenge was to furnish the selected basement apartment, which offered only a bed, single chair and small kitchen table. Other memorable tasks included the not too subtle demand to sample the traditional Southern food, grits (tastes like they ground the box that it came in and added butter) and feverishly trying to learn all the three-hundred odd names of athletic department staff, coaches, fellow athletic trainers, managers, eminent alumni and the male and female student athletes from all the various sports teams.

Due to the dominance of the football team, Mark's primary assignment was the day-to-day coverage needs for injury prevention and management for the football team. In the winter, Mark was primarily assigned to basketball, including road travel and during the spring Mark covered the needs of track and field. While some athletic trainers find track and field coverage uninspiring, Mark gradually learned to enjoy working with the nuances of overuse injuries and the frequent need to rehabilitate musculo-tendinous injuries back to full out efforts in a safely graded manner. Being a citizen-runner himself, Mark began to identify with many of the psychological needs of the runners. Frequently, a regimen of simple rest was not the acceptable treatment answer. Presumably, rest is a four-letter word to most competitive athletes.

The demands of the job quickly escalated into multiple responsibilities which Mark thought was awesome. On the second day on the job, Mark met a huge, towering and sleekly muscled athlete and overwhelmed by his size, assumed he must be a pro football player back to school for summer workouts, "Hey, man, I'm Mark, so where do you play?" Mark greeted the fellow. "Hi, are you the new assistant trainer?" responded the fellow, smiling warmly, confidently.

"That's me!" replied Mark lamely. "Nice to meet you, Sir." The player said as extended his huge hand to shake. "I play O-line here for Tech. I'm Kent Hill. I came in to get a stretch on my hamstring and get taped for weight training." (This player was selected to the All-American team during his upcoming senior season, was later drafted by the now vacated Los Angeles Rams team of the NFL and had a stellar career as a lead blocker for the famed pro running back, Eric Dickerson.) (Figure 4.1)

Feeling rather embarrassed by his premature but accurate assumption about that player, Mark began to recognize the sheer magnitude of Division 1 football: the size of the budget, the size of the players and the sheer number of athletes. When compared to his prior experience with Division II and III collegiate athletic programs, Mark was impressed by this newly escalated level of organization. In fact, he was truly thrilled with the opportunity to work and learn in this exciting environment.

Furthermore on his second day at Georgia Tech, Mark received a call from the Athletic Director informing him that he would be assessing the injury of a "VIP" at some point during the afternoon. As promised, in the early afternoon the back door to the athletic training opened with a flourish, and an entourage of men in business suits entered.

Led by the Athletic Director and the Head Sports Information Director, was a large black man walking protectively beside a smaller, distinguished looking black man dressed in a silky stylish warm-up suit. New to town, but not oblivious to his new environment, Mark instantly recognized the man as the Mayor of Atlanta, the honorable Andrew Young! *Holy crap*, thought Mark, *when they say VIP around here, they really mean it! This is awesome, my second day here and I'm treating the Mayor of Atlanta, how cool !*

The treatment and the interaction with the Mayor was most successful and Mark's career dreams were glowing brilliantly now! However, that initial euphoria was soon dulled by the grind of two-a-day practices was in full swing: a blur of fatigue, challenges and non-stop activity for all associated with a football program. The injury list mounts up as these training days pass, particularly among the uninitiated freshmen players who are desperately trying to adjust to the newly intense level of training and competition. These freshmen are lining up against bigger, faster and more skilled players who despite being teammates, right now are focused on protecting their own positions against these highly touted, but wholly unproven newcomers.

Some of the freshmen adjust and progress immediately, impressing the coaches to earn coveted playing time; others take time to gradually develop their positional skills; while still others become red-shirted due to injury. Sadly, a few forlorn souls leave the program, being unable to cope with the level of play, unable to abide by team rules or intolerant or unprepared of the impending academic challenges of college studies. This was always a somber moment for Mark, having to witness the fresh brave dreams of these young athletes crumble into dust and to share the pain of their embarrassment, defeat and dejection as they returned home to their proud families, friends and old classmates, ridden with the yoke of failure.

Described by stark statistical terms, this is merely the one in sixty rule being displayed. It has been calculated that only one-in-sixty high school football players advance to playing at Division 1 teams, and then again, the natural skill attrition reduces the successful collegiate stars to a one-in-sixty chance of playing in the NFL. This de-selection process illustrates the cruel nature of an "athletic survival of the fittest" (or at least, the least injured athletes). As a means of comparison to other grueling physical tests, the success ratio of Navy Seals is about 13%.Most amazingly of all, the odds of Chinese female gymnasts being selected to Olympic or World Cup competition is six *out of one million* potential Class nine or ten gymnasts who are capable of international success. Now **that** poses a serious, almost stifling pressure to perform for their country!

With the arrival of the opening game day, one of the

payoffs for all the pre-season hard work and sacrifices is realized in the thrilling form of the bus procession racing toward the stadium. Comprised of three new, air-conditioned, luxury tour buses (one each for the offense, the defense and for VIPs / staff) the cordon is led by the speeding motorcycle and state patrol escort, streaming through the night-lit streets of Columbia, SC. The blue lights of the police vehicles reflect mysteriously against passing palmetto trees and magnolias in the humid September darkness. With pomp we have arrived at the huge confines of Williams-Brice stadium filled with the pulsating, vibrating crowd noises. Entering the field under the gleaming, bright lights is a striking eye-opener for Mark. *Yes, this is the big time;* muses Mark, feeling more excited than nervous.

Tonight's contest is Georgia Tech's 1977 opening game against the threatening South Carolina Gamecocks, steeped with team speed on both sides of the ball. On a more minor note, it is also Mark's debut as an athletic trainer for a major college football game, and he is proud to wear the gold and white uniform of the coaching staff and more than a little pumped to provide the best and immediate care for any injuries that may occur! Bring it on, baby!

As future football seasons unfold, Mark remains enthralled by the speed, the precision and the sirens of the police escorts racing toward stadiums for college football, for both home and away games. It's the greatest way to travel and enjoy the journey, an exciting emotional charge-up preparation for the game, combining speed, celebrity and command of the road. These motorcades may reach speeds of 80-90 mph, dependent, of course, on road conditions and the numbers of turns on a selected route. But regardless of the city setting, the cops love turning up the speed when possible and it's alright with Mark, standing at his customary position at the front of the defensive team bus, "on the ready" to jump out and begin preparations for taping and stretching the players.

The throngs of reverent opposing fans that line the streets are also an amusing sidelight. As the buses cruise by, they often raise their arms to wave or their middle fingers to salute; all the while cheering their verbal well wishes and holding placards, encouraging us to visit hot places. Nonetheless, the bus motorcades are truly a top of the line, unforgettable travel experience!

The Georgia Tech position was a fantastic learning experience for Mark, punctuated with fun, funny and dramatic moments. Mark's first two seasons were filled with team travel, long days in the athletic training room, rapidly improved taping skills and an enforced depth of knowledge about classic sports injuries.(Figure 4.2) The ability to tape an ankle fast (under five minutes) is a criteria for a skilled athletic trainer, but Mark had refined his manual skill to perform the smooth, unwrinkled and snug tape job in only two minutes! (Figure 4.3)

There were definite highs and lows for the Tech sports teams, though. These highs and lows can be encapsulated in events when the GT football team collided with one of the powerhouse teams of that era, the Notre Dame Irish. In 1978, GT traveled to South Bend, IN. to face the undefeated, top-ranked Irish on their homecoming. Georgia Tech was also ranked in the top ten and felt the sting of disrespect in being scheduled as the opponent for their homecoming game!

The day began as a cloudy, gloomy fall day with a barren feeling due to the leafless trees and brown grass of the area. The gloom continued into the fabric of the game, and so did the measure of disrespect. As the team buses approached the gate, the elderly gate guard took his time examining the buses, despite the obvious arrival time on the itinerary. As he finally, slowly and grudgingly, swung the gates open, he stepped back so he was in full view of the buses, bowed up his back and gave several obscene gestures pumping his left forearm across his raised, bent right elbow and smiled insolently. *This is going to be a challenge!* thought Mark, with growing realization of its magnitude.

The players (eighty on this traveling squad) and the athletic trainers, managers, physicians and coaches crowded into what appeared to be a sardine can of a locker room, old, decrepit and compromised on one entire wall by the indentation of a bleacher row imprinted into the ceiling. Due to the shortage of lockers, players were forced to share stalls and the taller players had to walk hunched over to avoid head injuries with the low menacing cement ceiling.

In the midst of the crowding and the commotion of pre-game preparations, Mark and the athletic training staff set about to tape the players with varied skilled applications, being cautious not pull the tape excessively and round-house an unsuspecting player in the nose. Fortunately, the cramped and deplorable conditions were not responsible for any pre-game locker room mishaps.

Midway during the pre-game period, the lack of respect was ramped up even higher as the huge and famous Notre Dame band pumped out fight songs positioned directly above our locker room, with the cement stair acting as a huge vibrating speaker Although, Mark is a fan of big-band, brass music, this situation was nearly intolerable. The sound rained down on the unsuspecting GT team, fostering a torment usually reserved for terror and criminal suspects during interrogations.

Most certainly, when a team travels they expect to be treated roughly, but not at this level of affront by a rich, historically religious based and successful school like Notre Dame. In fact in all his days as a competitive gymnast in high school and college, Mark had never witnessed such a worn-out, embarrassing locker room set-up! But the Fighting Irish had yet another little jab to the respect ribs. In a vocal flurry, Mark was summoned by the head student trainer whose job including counting the provided towels and placing some on the team benches for game use." Mark, I have counted the towels twice and there are only fifty!" sputtered the exasperated twenty year old student athletic trainer.(the standard towel allowance for visiting teams was 250 in Mark's experience!)

"OK, man, I'll go over to their locker room and get it straightened out," responded Mark, initially considering this as a mere oversight. When Mark entered the Notre Dame locker room, he was amazed at the beauty and splendor of the open cage lockers and wooden benches, plush carpet and pristine setting of the athletic training room. Mark questioned his counterpart, the Notre Dame assistant athletic trainer about the towel shortage and was brusquely dismissed with; "Ah, yeah, that's what you get." "Surely you jest, we have eighty players and staff and we need 250 towels!" countered Mark in a sarcastic tone. "Well, sorry I can't help ya." came the reply.

Mark found this attitude to be most incredulous. Athletic trainers are generally a closely knit order of fellow professionals who understand each other's world and always attempt to support one another. Mark's amazement at this wholly unprofessional stance was quietly and quickly flooding into anger. "OK, dude, now that I have your name as the one responsible I want you to think about the fact that you are visiting our place next year and I have a great memory for important facts and I assure that you will get fifty towels if I don't have another damn two-hundred towels that are clean and properly folded in our locker room within the next five minutes." Mark snapped, scowling and quickly left the opulent locker room setting.

In magical fashion, the student athletic trainer soon after announced with glee that two-hundred towels had just been delivered!

The game started with two quick touchdowns by the Irish and the Georgia Tech defense was not adjusting well. However, suddenly the Georgia Tech offensive scheme began to click and the halftime score, 20-14 left the Tech team hopeful of second half success.

The GT team was victimized by two early second half turnovers leading to easy touchdowns, causing the flood gates to open for the Irish offense led by a pretty darn good quarterback, Joe Montana. The score ballooned to 55-14 in the early fourth quarter. There was no luck of the Irish involved; as the score mounted, the Tech players were confused, often injured, exhausted and fully humiliated. When the deciding touchdown was scored, the heavens cleared completely, and like a mystical omen, the sunbeams glinted majestically off the famed Golden Dome of the campus.

Oh, but the degradation was not yet complete. In the late fourth quarter, on a fourth down and long situation on the Georgia Tech 38 yard line, Notre Dame called a time-out. The team lined up in normal offensive formation, which in this case was distastefully offensive, faked a run up the middle and then the quarterback rolled out and threw a long pass to the end-zone and scored yet another touchdown. The final, sickening score was 69-14!.

It was a grimly depressing airline flight back to Atlanta, doubly so, because this was the only college football game that Mark's parents were ever able to attend watching him working as the athletic trainer on the sideline. And although it is decidedly not a Christian precept, thoughts of retaliation and retribution danced around the margins of Mark's mind, and we would have to believe, in the minds of many young GT football players and seasoned coaches.

Just as sports' competitive lows are endured as painful memories, the highs must be celebrated and fond stories are formed. A sort of psychic balance is played out over time. A truly glorious high was to unfold on a brilliant fall day in 1980 in Atlanta GA. This time Notre Dame was the visiting team for the annual football match-up with Georgia Tech. Once again, Notre Dame was top rated and expectant of an easy victory! Hours later, fish of all sizes were raining from the heavens covering the brilliant green Astroturf carpet of Grant Field on the visitors sideline.

Although it was not the Biblical end of the world, it may have seemed like it for the shocked Notre Dame team as the score board blinked the final score, GT 3, ND 3. Wow, the Georgia Tech team had rallied behind heavy emotion and tied the mighty, favored Irish without throwing a single pass in the game. With stinging impact, the ecstatic student section had prepared for this upset, stocking up on fish at the local market to make a wild smelly statement of disrespect and poor sportsmanship. How glorious their statement seemed in the fading light of that triumphant day! But there wasn't much glory for the assembled campus police and state patrol officers who needed to restore order. Moreover, Mark's friends on the grounds crew were not feeling very triumphant as they cleared the slippery, smelly mess left behind.

Mark's career with Georgia Tech was interrupted by a wonderful opportunity to become a professional sports team athletic trainer with the Atlanta Chiefs in 1978. The Atlanta Chiefs were established as an expansion team in the professional soccer league of that era, the North American Soccer League — (known as the N.A.S.L.) Mark would return to Georgia Tech however, in 1981, in a new hybrid role as an assistant athletic trainer and the director of an in-house rehab/ treatment center housed within the athletic department.

Mark's second tenure with GT involved working with two new head football coaches and an exciting, frenetic, prematurely grey haired basketball coach, Bobby Cremins. Serving as Bobby Cremins first athletic trainer at Georgia Tech was a memorable time as the basketball program was primed for national attention with skilled new players who achieved ALL-ACC status, went to the Final Four in the NCAA tournament and eventually became pros: Mark Price, John Salley, Duane Ferrell, Dennis Scott and others.

Also during 1981, Mark founded a new private practice physical therapy clinic (the very first inside the Atlanta metro ring) called STEP of Atlanta, Inc. (the acronym for Sports Therapy and Exercise Prescription) that specialized in sports medicine rehabilitation and provided with community and high school game coverage. Moreover, Mark was becoming more polished, recognizable and in demand as a continuing education speaker throughout the US. As for all medical professions, both the athletic training and physical therapy professions require continuing education units (CEU's) to maintain their valid licenses. Mark's career was now in full swing and this total immersion demanded sixty to seventy hour work weeks for the decade of the 1980s. In retrospect, this period of "going fast" provided a wonderful boost of income that his father had predicted many years before. At last!

Mark's intense practicum of rehabilitation for one of the most commonly disabling sports injuries, the torn ACL (anterior cruciate ligament) in the knee, provided a rich area for his clinical business. Mark's expertise working with ACL injuries was cemented in his first year at Georgia Tech when he covered a Junior Varsity contest against South Carolina that resulted in an unheard of seven ACL tears by game's end. Although a tragic injury total for a single football game, that day emblazoned a deep understanding of ACL injury mechanisms and acute recognition that formed the basis for specialization in the prolonged post-surgical rehab stages for this injury. Once again, a change of plane had developed this one intrinsic to Mark's career development. Based on a patient chart audit in 2000, Mark had successfully rehabilitated over 1,200 ACL tears – mostly for athletes who returned to their respective sports.

Mark's final year at Georgia Tech was 1990, when the

GT football culminated a magical undefeated season, powered by a team blessed with great defensive speed and won
the mythical national championship (some claim that it was
a co-championship with Colorado). Mark has great pride in
his contribution to that team and has a championship ring
to savor that achievement. (Fig.4.4)

Folllowing the Georgia Tech tenure, Mark's career em-
phasized clinical physical therapy in multiple professional
settings: as a clinical director for a corporate Fortune 500
company practice, as the sports medicine program director
at Eisenhower Medical Center in Rancho Mirage CA and
clinical director for a large outpatient orthopedic practice
in metro Atlanta. The money had definitely arrived, accompanied by a renewal of the concept that salary and job
satisfaction can be mutually exclusive conditions.

Figure 1.1 Railway Motors Pump Car

Figure 3.1 Gymnastic splits on floor exercise

Figure 3.2 Finishing a 10K

Figure 3.3 Kerri Strug warming up for a gymnastic rotation – center foreground

Figure 4.1 Kent Hill with Mark—Mark is on the right!!!

Figure 4.2 Pre-game on the famed Rambling Wreck car.

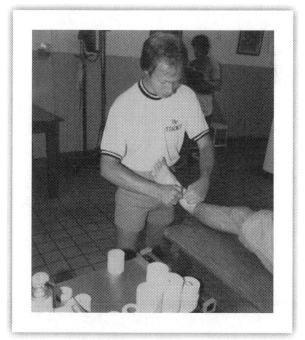

Figure 4.3 Pre-game taping session.

Figure 4.4 The Georgia Tech 1990 Football national Championship ring.

Figure 6.1 The Crew from Freshman Year

CHAPTER 5.

Pictures on My Wall

The handshake is the socially accepted American gesture for meeting and greeting. It also carries weight as an expression of touch in friendship. In business, it signifies a measure of respect, and when an agreement has been reached, it culminates as a pledge of trust and a moment of conclusion. Each social situation dictates the appropriate amount of manual pressure and grip force. For males, a forceful pumping of elbow flexion may be expected, but in contrast, when males shake the hand of a lady, a gentle, finger only grasp is often considered most desirable.

Today, standing in the oppressive August heat and humidity of this Atlanta summer day, the two hands joined in a cordial shake were moist with sweat. But this handshake was different, vibratory in nature. Beyond the world-wide notoriety of the person whose hand Mark he was shaking, causing him to feel slightly shaky, this hand was famous for it's devastating power, blinding speed and maddeningly, playful rope-a-dope circles. The owner of this hand had been very busy the last few days, raising an emblematic flame to initiate the Atlanta Olympic Games, then serving as a Goodwill Ambassador to countless dignitaries and admiring fans from around the globe, shaking hands while holding back on the tremors imposed by Parkinson disease. Throughout all the preceding activities he maintained a smile, despite the mask-like restriction of his facial muscles, just as he was smiling now at Mark.

"Mr. Ali, I am very honored to meet you, and I hope this heat isn't too much for you." said Mark as they ceased the handshake. *Of all the many handshakes in my career,* thought Mark, *that was the biggest hand of all! Just huge* " No, ahh, I like the heat, I have my water here, you see." "Sir, the lighting of the flame, was breathtaking, Thank you for serving this role." replied Mark, at least, that's what he recalls, because the state of his awe may well have blurred his memory. As Muhammed nodded in understanding, Mark's former colleague and friend from the days of the soccer Atlanta Chiefs, Mike interrupted, counseling in his gentle, diplomatic and unassuming manner, "Mr. Ali, it's time for the luncheon, I'll help you inside" Muhammed merely nodded a goodbye and he rose, so slowly from the chair and Mark's meeting was over. But the vibration of the handshake was still present.

Friends are so important on many levels, sometimes opening doors to opportunities that may never have otherwise existed and so it was on this momentous, hot day in 1996 for Mark. Having cleared the extensive security line at Mark's Olympic Gymnastic Venue, he had checked in all scheduled staff, reviewed the supplies in the Athletic Training Room at the Georgia Dome, when the phone rang. It was his friend, Mike, who had served as the SID (Sports

Information Director) for the Atlanta Chiefs Soccer Team. Being two young guys in their respective first professional team jobs, they often worked on projects together and traveled to all team away games, so a natural friendship and mutual trust developed.

Mike was selected as a media liaison for several ongoing projects during the Olympics to coordinate athlete interviews. On this particular day, Mark had planned on checking in with Mike at the Olympic Village media center, just to see how things were coordinated. Mark's zero clearance badge allowed him access to any venue and every event, so gaining access was no issue, despite the tight security measures at entrance gates.

"Hey, Mark, I won't be able to show you around today. A conflict has come up with a VIP media luncheon and I am already here to coordinate all the attendees." explained Mike. "No sweat" replied Mark, now considering where he would go out of the venue today for lunch. "But I have something even better. If you can get over here by 12 noon, I will arrange for you to meet privately with Muhammed Ali for a minute or so." "Jeez, really? I am on my way, right now!" said Mark. As he looked at the time, 11:10, Mark fretted with the realization, *this was going to be tight.* "OK, meet me on the North side of the Village at Gate K," responded Mike with urgency.

Despite being only three miles apart, the two venues were separated by tremendous traffic congestion and delays, the public transportation trains (MARTA ™) were packed at every stop and the only possible solution was a taxi. But taxis were at a premium at every designated stop! Thinking back to his college days, a bike would have been the perfect answer on this day! Mark dashed through the Georgia Dome to the nearest taxi stand and miraculously caught a taxi just letting off his passenger, bribed the driver for a speedy route and made it to the designated gate by 11:52. And there sitting under a tree in a plastic chair with Mike by his side, was the legend, perhaps, the most famous athlete of all time, Muhammed Ali.

Not to be construed as a groupie, a gossip columnist or heaven forbid, a paparazzi, Mark was nevertheless intrigued by the many chance meetings he had with the notable, famous and the fortunate citizens of America. These encounters occurred during travel, during airport waiting periods and during the patient-client relationships that manifested through the decades. Although proud of his participation and guidance for the successful outcome of famed patients, his memories of these episodes was essentially reminiscent of a famed chef, whose restaurant is frequented by celebrities from the arts, business and sports worlds. As time passes, the chef is seen photographed, smiling with these notable patrons and they gradually take their place displayed on the walls of the restaurant.

Fame is a capricious condition. It may be fleeting and fluky, deserved and enduring, universal or local in effect. Whatever the slant, we all seem to be drawn to fame in our varied, personal ways. For Mark, his encounters with famous and renowned people throughout his career were abundant, and consequently, we will relate a select number of these experiential vignettes.

Mark structured and directed the injury rehab for athletes who soon after resumed competition and achieved pinnacles in their sports:

- Vernon Forrest – who won the world middleweight boxing championship
- Antonio McKay – a 1982 Olympic track star who set the world record time in the 400 meter race soon after rehab
- Dave Pasanella – a competitive power lifter, who set the world record in the 1980's in the squat lift during ongoing physical therapy.

(Regrettably, both Mr. Forrest and Mr. Pasanella are deceased. This passage is offered as a respectful tribute to their memories.)

In like fashion, Mark also treated several notable entertainers over his career: country singer Willie Nelson, Harry Shearer, famous for the movie *Spinal Tap* and the Simpson's TV show fame and the musician Moby. Rather, embarrassingly, Mark treated Moby prior to a concert show in Atlanta, having no recognition of his music or his career. But Mark's curiosity about this fellow was piqued when he claimed to be a rock music performer that was headed out on a world tour. Upon completing his work week with his treatment and leaving the facility to head home, Mark stopped at a book store for reading material and shockingly enough, encountered a picture of his just departed patient on the cover of Newsweek, staring back at him!

Airports are ideal places to observe people and because of the endless waiting time during extensive air travel, you will have many opportunities. By their very nature, they serve as a social gathering spot for the hurried, the harried and the bored. Citizens of all sort pass by the airport gates and the human condition is on steady parade. You will see the classy and classless, the sassy and the clueless blending with the over-dressed and highly stressed. Seemingly, the universal travel attire is black, but there are endless permutations on this basic theme.

Mark fondly recalls the young man in LAX (Los Angeles Airport) who seemed to be presenting his own Clockwork Orange[10] reprise. Adorned in orange shorts, backward tilted baseball cap and orange tank shirt, his sunglasses had orange frames and his knee high, orange and white striped candy cane socks were housed inside, yeah, you guessed right, orange Converse All-Stars. But wait, let's not overlook the orange fashion backpack riding low on his left shoulder. The whole ensemble was a most unusual look, but then again, what fashion statement would you expect in La La Land?

Airports are also great places to run into people, both literally and figuratively. Literally, when running down the long arched terminals of Chicago's O'Hare to catch the last late night flight to LAX caused by a delightful forty-five minute herding of slow-moving people in the half mile long security line; weaving around with endless turns like the human dragon parade celebrating the Chinese New Year.

Also, literally, when Mark was running around the blank wall of a connecting flight in Atlanta, to turn blindly and smack headlong into a famous golf teacher, David Ledbetter, who looked for the briefest instant poised like he was going to take a swing rather than correct one. Mark offered his brief, hurried, "excuse me, sir" and realizing this was no time for the autograph in this instance, Mark continued running to his next gate.

---

[10] 1980 movie by Stanley Kubrick.

Although it seems that Mark has reasonably good looks (at least his mother and maybe a few college girls think so), it escapes him why so many people mistake him for someone else when he travels. Both random fellow travelers and even a few celebrities, have given him the overly obvious stare-down, or have actually *asked for his autograph* or even more incredibly offered him concert tickets to their upcoming performance.

Waiting for a flight in Atlanta, fifteen years ago, Mark was sitting on the end seat of a row of chairs facing the terminal hallway and reading the paper. Mark was increasingly distracted by a funny, sort of hissing sound nearby. Being somewhat puzzled, Mark dropped the newspaper suddenly, to witness two little girls kneeling near him, and then they suddenly ran away across the aisle. Now back to the newspaper, he was interrupted by a lady's voice asking;

"Ahh, sir, my girls are big fans of yours, could you please give them an autograph?" While not completely unfamiliar with celebrity, Mark found this request both amusing and puzzling, "Sure thing," proclaimed Mark, as the girls presented little note books. Mark signed his name and handed back the books. The mother looked at his signature and becoming red-faced suddenly barked out, "You must really think your something, it's a damn shame that you can't even give a child a real autograph!!!"

This was sort of like an aberration of "What's My Line?", only in this case, it was more like "Who am I now?" Obviously, the timing wasn't right to have a conversation with the incensed lady to determine who Mark was supposed to be. Besides, the lady stormed away, grabbed her girls and disappeared down the terminal hallway.

On another instance, returning from teaching a course in Cincinnati, Mark checked in at the desk for his flight and caught the gaze of a man standing nearby. Balding and heavy-set, this man nodded at Mark, but was not familiar to him. When boarding was called, Mark inadvertently fell in line behind the man and was able to read the electronic display from his boarding pass which read Cross, C. *Could that really be the Grammy winning musician with the Number 1 hit son, Sailing?* thought Mark, with a building sense of curiosity.

As Mark found his assigned seat in coach, he passed the man, who was seated in first class, who nodded again. After the seatbelt sign was turned off, the man walked quickly back to Mark's aisle seat, stopped and quietly said; "I'm sorry that you missed my concert last night. Man, I didn't know that you were in town or I would have gotten you tickets!" A little tongue tied and perplexed, Mark replied with a smile "Yeah, no problem, no problem at all, but maybe next time." *Once again, the theme of "Who Am I now?"* crossed Mark's mind. The musician Christopher Cross apparently recognized Mark from some misperceived appearance. And yet another most curious airport event had just occurred.

#39

In the presidential election of 1978, a former small-town Georgia peanut farmer who had served as Georgia's governor, ran a resplendent campaign and surprisingly was elected as America's 39th President. As a former student at

Georgia Tech, Jimmy Carter maintained contact with both the school and the Athletic Department during his tenure. His and Mark's path would soon collide in a most happenstance manner.

During 1978, the Georgia Tech football team was scheduled to play Navy in Annapolis. It was arranged that the entire traveling team and dignitaries were invited to meet with the President and receive a tour of the White House. The anticipated November Friday arrived, a sunny, warm day in the Capitol. As the gates opened to the South Lawn portico, this was a breathtaking opportunity for Mark. He felt especially proud to be American. During the tour, his interest in literature and history exceeded his common sense, as he drifted away from the large group to view the setting of the famed Presidential library.

A soft but firm voice startled Mark from behind, stating; "It's probably best that you catch up with the group, the Secret Service frowns on unattended visits." smiled Rosalyn Carter, as always the gracious Southern First Lady. "I'm really sorry, ma'am" muttered Mark, filled with embarrassment, "I'll catch up with the group. Thanks." Hence, Mark strode quickly down the central hallway to join the main group, lamenting on his impertinence, but inwardly thrilled with his private moment with the First Lady.

As an athletic trainer for Georgia Tech, Mark's game day duties included the supervision of loading the defensive team bus and checking that all were seated. Upon completing the White House tour, there was a lot of commotion among the coaches and players to get photos of the grounds and to thank the various White House staff for their hospitality. Consequently, amidst the press, White House staff, security people and all the Georgia Tech entourage; Mark was having a difficult time assuring an accurate head count for his bus.

With his frustration level probably visible, Mark was fully focused on finishing the loading, fretting that he would make a mistake, envisioning that the morning newspapers were going to run a headline like; <u>Georgia Tech Football Player Left Behind at the White House</u>. *Yes, that would be really bad*, mused Mark as he was suddenly surprised by someone standing right next to him, smiling. It was the President himself, cordially seeing the team off. "It sure looks like you have a tough job, there son." the President remarked, affably.

Momentarily at a loss for words, Mark shook his head no, responding, "Mr. President, nothing to compare to your job!" "Well, you can see I have a lot of help. Good luck with the game tomorrow. I will be rooting for you in the first half." "Thank you, Sir!" *Why just the first half* ? wondered Mark, learning later that President Carter was also a Navy man, and would be sitting on the Navy side for the second half. Well, sometimes image and politics trump the sports concerns, as in this case.

Much later in Mark's career, while serving as one of the managers for the athletic training staff during the Olympics, this situation repeated itself, with another President, Bill Clinton. As very strong sports fans, the Clintons planned to attend a team gymnastic competition and preceding the visit, the Secret Service was tasked to inspect and "sanitize" the entire Georgia Dome, with special attention to all the cabinets and multiple supplies housed within the athletic training room.

During this process, the athletic training room was closed to all athletes and coaches, while sternly guarded by a Secret Service agent, replete with the standardized blue blazer, white shirt and ear piece. Unfortunately for Mark, the competitive sessions and practices proceeded regardless of imposed Secret Service activity and Mark had several stand-offs with the agents when he needed to enter the training room for necessary supplies. At the time, it seemed like a true pain in the butt, but take a hit for the President!

The following year during basketball season, the city of Atlanta was looking forward to a scheduled visit from President Carter. Mark was now the acting athletic trainer for the basketball team and on this particular day was treating several student athletes alone in the athletic training room. For a week-day near to the lunch hour, it was uncharacteristically quiet time in the athletic training room.

Suddenly in a rush of activity, the back door to the training room opened, with a group of well dressed men entering. First the SID (Sports Information Director), the Athletic Director, an unknown man in a suit, then with a flourish, the President of the United States, flanked by his security detail. As the group approached Mark, the training room became even quieter, filled with a shocked, awed silence (a definite rarity in collegiate athletic training rooms).

The Athletic Director started the surprise visit by announcing proudly to Mark: "We have just arranged to have the President attend our next season's basketball game against Navy, and during our discussion, President Carter remembered you from our football visit and wanted to know if you would be on the basketball trip also." Disregarding the political preference a person had or personal opinion they held regarding President Carter, he was widely known for his astounding, crisp memory for people and names. Now on this day, a most incredible thing, *the President remembered Mark?*

"It's good to see you again, President Carter. I'll see if I'm the Athletic Trainer for that trip." The Athletic Director quickly interjected, "We'll see to that, Mark." "Well, I will look forward to seeing you then and I would like you to get me two tickets for the game One of my staff will arrange the rest of the details." responded the President "I will see to it, Sir." concluded Mark in his most official sounding voice.

The group quickly exited the training room to proceed with the remainder of the President's busy day with the planned meetings, leaving the several athletes in the training room in shocked disbelief. After a brief pause, the solitary football player in attendance asked incredulously; "You really know the President ?" With a sly grin, Mark responded facetiously, "Oh yeah, were tight, just like this !" gesturing with upraised, crossed index and middle fingers.

Mark made the trip with the basketball team to play Navy, and as it had been previously arranged, Mark excused himself from his pre-game team duties for a moment and rather than leaving the tickets at a will-call window, Mark personally delivered the two tickets to a smiling Jimmy Carter accompanied by his Secret Service agent at the predetermined gate at precisely, 12:55 for the 1 pm game. The President's express directive was to pass through the turnstiles with a ticket in hand, just as all the other fans were required to do! Needless to say, the ticket takers, nearby ushers and food vendors were all looking at Mark as if he were straight from the moon. Who was this guy, anyway, handing the President of the United States tickets to the game?

Rushing through the crowded halls of the arena, Mark returned to the Georgia Tech locker room and was immediately questioned pointedly by the Head Coach, "Where were you?" In his sincerest voice, Mark responded "I just delivered the game tickets to President Carter as he had requested. He wished you good luck, Coach, and he is sitting on our sideline in the first half."

With casual distraction, the Coach merely nodded and walked to the arena entrance. As the years passed, Mark forgot the winner of the game, but felt like a winner because of his personal contact with the President of the United States.

Bart Conner

As one of the most decorated American male gymnasts of all time, Bart Conner, Bart competed on the Men's Olympic teams from 1976 to 1984 in addition to winning an NCAA championship. During the 1996 Olympics, Bart also served as the TV analyst for the gymnastic competition, and periodically visited with Mark and the athletic training staff. After three weeks of competition, Mark was well acquainted with Bart, and his fellow announcer, John Tesh. Earlier in the year, Bart had also married another gymnastic legend, Nadia Comaneci from Romania who was the first female gymnast to score a perfect ten in gymnastic competition.

At the end of the gymnastics competition, the audiences were treated to a special champion's gala production which featured performances from all the male and female medalists as well as exhibitions of the world champions in trampoline and tumbling. A truly exciting night staged with dramatic music and special spotlights The capacity crowd was thunderous in it's applause, which regrettably Mark could only hear as a vague vibration at a distance. As part of Mark's duties, he was tasked to inventory and supervise the secure packing of supplies and materials as the gymnastic venue was closed.

Rushing through his duties, Mark was excited to finally get to see a little of the concluding exhibition action, and forging his way to the floor level chairs for officials found his way through the darkness of the arena to a last remaining empty chair. Due to his gymnastic background, Mark was thrilled to watch the final event of the evening, a spirited and competitive series of tumbling passes performed on singular, long strip of runner mats. As each world class tumbler performed more explosive and difficult passes down the mat, it seemed that every gymnast that followed would surpass the height, speed and difficulty on their next pass. The final tumbler was greeted with a frenzied crescendo of standing applause and Mark found himself reflexively high fiving the man sitting next to him, who was smiling with appreciation: Bart Conner!

Bart asked Mark; "Hey, you look like you know tumbling." "Yup, I was a high school and college gymnast and loved to tumble." Bart quickly responded nodding his recollection, "Yes, so did I. It was great fun." Encouraged by this friendly exchange, Mark felt comfortable asking Bart a question that many people had wondered about.

"Bart, can you tell why you chose to get married in

Romania?" Bart's reply was thoughtful, unhesitating and concise; "Well I could have gotten married in the small A-frame church in Norman (Bart's Oklahoma college town) with a lot of expense, or in my case, I could be married in a State ceremony as honored celebrities in the elaborate Parliament House of Romania, and all of the expenses were paid." "So, what would you have done?" "Ah, thanks for telling me Bart, yeah, I would have done the same thing."

As the full floor lights came on and the music began to play a concluding piece signifying the end to the exhibition, Mark and Bart shook hands and said their farewells. This exchange served as a glowing culmination to Mark's active involvement with competitive gymnastics and in retrospect, provided a perfect ending to a signature event in Mark's career.

Ted Turner

Famous for his many business and social facets, Ted Turner is a most influential and interesting man. It could be said that his media empire projected the charm of Atlanta as a Southern treasure and promoted a worldwide view of Atlanta as a cultural and business hub. As a pioneer in cable television, and an active owner of professional sports franchises, he was admittedly proud of bringing back a professional soccer franchise to Atlanta. The Atlanta Chiefs of the North American Soccer League began business in the spring of 1979. Serving as the closely held owner of the team, Mr. Turner became Mark's ultimate boss during Mark's first opportunity as an athletic trainer for a professional sports franchise. In fact, for the first year of the team's existence, Mr. Turner actually manually signed Mark's paycheck!

Whereas Mr. Turner was usually more focused on the big picture of his multiple business projects; he notoriously left the operational details to others in his business .However, during the preparation build-up to the Chiefs first game in Washington DC in the old Robert F. Kennedy (RFK) stadium, Ted was seen frequently in attendance of team practices. Thus, it was not surprising that Ted's busy travel schedule and hectic demands, still allowed him to accompany the team to Washington for their first game. He even stayed with the team at the Watergate Hotel, famed for both its unique curved architecture and historic political events swirling around the Presidency of Richard Nixon.

During away games, Mark would precede the team bus to the stadium to prepare the locker room for team uniforms and to set up the locker room training room area. As Mark moved all of the team travel trunks and bags from the hotel to a waiting taxi for the trip to the stadium, he noticed the sideward glances of the bell captains as they assisted him in loading. The undivided attention of the bell captains to a professional athletic trainer was both flattering and helpful, but always predicated on their expectation of a generous tip.

Following repeated glances of the bell captains to Mark's left, he noticed a tall, well dressed man standing near the hotel frontage, looking in his direction. It was Ted Turner. Well before he had the Atlanta Braves baseball stadium named in his honor, or when he founded his restaurant group, Ted's Montana Grill; Mr. Turner was reputed as one of the wealthiest men in America. Due to his television notoriety he was automatically recognizable in the public forum. Mark caught his glance and waved a hello.

As Mark handed out the tips, he felt the presence of someone standing near to him on the curb. Turning around, he was now face to face with Mr. Turner, who was smiling and offering his hand in greeting. As noted earlier, Ted was a big picture man and although he knew Mark's role with the team, he could never recall his name.

"Hey, Mr. Turner, how are you today?" offered Mark. "We are all excited about the game, are you heading to the stadium?" came his response.

"Yes, I'm on my way, do you want to ride with me? questioned Mark, with uncertainty. "Ahhh, well no, I have some business that has come up and I'm going to have to head back to Atlanta right now." responded Ted. "Well, I'm sorry to hear that. We can drop you off at the airport if you like. It's right on the way." Mark was referring to the central location of Washington National (now renamed Reagan) airport en-route to the former RFK stadium. Flights taking off from this airport routinely provide the passenger with a high speed thrill as they accelerate to gain a rapid ascent over the nearby adjoining bridge.

In the meantime, the cabbie is standing anxiously at the trunk of his cab, waiting impatiently and now a crowd of bell boys and hotel doorman are observing this conversation with obvious interest, but trying to act casual.

"Ahhh, no thanks, but I didn't plan on this trip and I'm wondering if you could give me some cab fare." Now this is an incredible situation, one of the richest men in America and Mark's boss is asking for some money. *Wow, could this really be happening*, thought Mark "Sure thing, Sir," as he reached into his billfold, offering a $50 bill, "Will this cover it?" "Yes, I really appreciate this and best of luck at the game. "No problem, Sir, it's your money. I hope you get your business settled." Mark's statement was received with a confused look on Ted's face. accompanied by his quick wave of goodbye as he walked toward another waiting cab.

After the game and return to Atlanta, Mark began to fill out his customary expense report for the trip, providing and itemizing receipts to support his cash advance depletion. Mark realized he faced a small dilemma. He obviously had not requested a receipt from Mr. Turner, and since this was a most unusual transaction, he decided to list it under miscellaneous – Cash advance: Mr. Turner cab fare. The unethical padding of business expense accounts probably occurs multiple times daily worldwide, and although this entry seemed over the top, it was undeniably true.

Three days later, when stopping at the team's corporate headquarters in the Stadium to check on supply deliveries, the main secretary informed him that the General Manager wanted to meet with him right now. Entering the GM's office, he was told to have a seat. Following a brief request about a specific player's injury progress, the GM quickly changed subjects and with an accusatory serious tone asked; "Now about your Washington expense report, do you expect me to believe this Ted Turner entry?" Sensing some serious accusation, Mark's reply was interrupted by the GM's sudden smirk and chuckle as he followed with the comment; "I'm just joking with you. Mr. Turner already told me how grateful he was for your help and wanted me to thank you for it." "Oh, like I said to him, it was his money." exhaling with a look of relief on his face. Mark has periodically grinned through the years when he has recalled lending money to one of the richest men in America.

Holy Cow!

February in the Southern California desert communities of Palm Springs and Rancho Mirage is hot: both with the weather and as the desirable destination for multitudes of snow birds that descend from myriad locations, like Chicago. For any Chicago baseball fan, particularly the Cubs faithful, Harry Caray was legendary for his voluminous and distinctive voice as the longtime radio/TV announcer. Like thousands of others, Harry Caray also enjoyed winter breaks in the desert.

With Harry's colorful rubric and stories, his most celebrated vocal out-bursts were the signature; **Hol-eee Cooww!** ; blasted forth with home runs, out-standing field plays or clutch hits during the game. Rumor has it that Harry liked to keep his throat well lubricated during games, which undoubtedly added to the fun(if not for him, then certainly for the fans who were listening).After teaching a course in nearby San Bernandino, Mark stayed on for a few days of winter warmth in Rancho Mirage.

On a Saturday night, Mark decided to have Italian food at his favorite place, Banducci's (now closed). Due to the large visiting crowds in town and this restaurant's popularity, Mark was offered the only remaining seat near the back room service bar in a dimly lighted booth. But a measure of destiny was at work this evening.

Mark was seated on the benches next to a couple whose

faces were hidden by the mammoth menus that were a trademark of this traditional place. As Mark considered his entrée choice, he was increasingly drawn to the distinctive, voluminous male voice next to him. *Where do I know that voice from?* wondered Mark, straining to focus and place a name with that distinctive voice.

Moments later the menus dropped down and the man sitting next to Mark lowered his glasses, peered at him and inquired in a friendly way, "So, what are *you* going to get?" The man's face was now instantly familiar, framed by the legendary trademark, oversized black horn rimmed glasses. And his voice was positively resonant :Mark was looking at Harry Caray!!! "Well, I think everything is good here, but I'm going with the pasta fra diavolo, how about you?" Lowering his voice, Mr. Caray announced with conviction, "I'm going to have those sausage and peppers."

Although Mark was not introduced to the lady sitting to Harry's right, it was presumably his wife and she immediately chided Harry with a grating voice; "Harry, you know you can't eat sausage and peppers!" To which Harry quickly responded, "Huh, a man can't even eat what he wants!"

In a conscious effort to avoid causing a public scene in the middle of his dinner, Mark merely nodded his silent agreement and the two men proceeded to discuss the restaurant and the wicked winter weather in Chicago prior to receiving their respective dinners. Harry had indeed ordered sausage and peppers. There was no mention of baseball or Harry's notoriety, just a bonding of two hungry men.

When he finished his meal, Mark rose and shook hands warmly with Harry as he proclaimed; "Sir, it was a pleasure talking with you and I love visiting Chicago, it's a great town just not in winter months. You and your wife enjoy your stay down here, and take care."

In a televised interview before his death in 1998, Harry described himself as a people person and stated, "the only thing to be is your natural self." Mark witnessed that essential personality trait that night in 1995. It was an unforgettable dining experience and he felt honored to enjoy a casual, uninterrupted conversation with the legend. Several times afterward, Mark wondered if Harry mentioned his conversation with *that nice young man* or maybe, if Harry simply suffered with digestive issues during his evening.

Although Mark seemed to have surprisingly frequent contact with the rich and famous, Mark felt most privileged and awed by the particular patient he treated for a tibial stress fracture. While neither rich nor famous, nor even fully qualified in his desired profession, Mark believed this patient symbolized the epitome of values in life: American patriotism and loyalty; team work and discipline and mental toughness.

For many years, Mark had been fascinated by the lore of the Navy SEALs, their reputation as warriors and the exquisite training that they endured. But in the 1990s, the details of their clan were rarely written about as was their pledge of secrecy. The publication of the amazing book, <u>Lone Survivor</u> [11], recounted a thrilling SEAL mission that led to the unfortunate death of the entire team, excluding the author. While this book was considered controversial

---

[11] Luttrell, Marcus. 2007 Lone Survivor. The Eyewitness Account of Operation Redwing and the Lost Heroes of Seal Team 10. Back Bay Books, New York.

in divulging SEAL tactics, the story inspired Mark with a great admiration for the heroes called SEALS. Mark was compelled to read many other available books regarding the Navy SEAL training, team work and creed.

Thus in 2008, it was a total surprise that a PT colleague of Mark, referred him a patient that was a SEAL candidate from the training base in Coronado Island near San Diego, which was described in detail in the Lone Survivor book. Faced with the physical intensity of their training, this patient named Ben, was a prospective Navy Seal who had been injured during the last stages of his BUDS training. Upon successful conclusion of the young Navy man's treatment, the interaction between Ben and Mark had fostered a mutual respect. Subsequently, Ben offered Mark a dream experience: Mark was invited to tour the Navy SEAL base in Coronado with Ben as his guide and sponsor, provided Mark could get down to San Diego.

Accentuated by the dry and sunny climate, the expansive beach on Coronado Island is annually picked among the finest in the world. Adjacent to the sandy shore stands the historic and elegant spires of the Hotel Del Coronado and nearby the shopping venues and restaurants on Orange Avenue beckon the visitors. However, all this sensory delight is muted and distant for the brave, committed men training and striving to become the elite Navy SEALS.

The Navy SEAL base adjoins the expanse of public beach. During his own prior running sessions on this beach zone, Mark had witnessed the small groups of muscled men running on the beach, clad in sweated T-shirts and sandy boots, struggling to maintain a set pace, not only for fitness, but to survive their long testing days.

And now, at this very exciting moment Mark was being escorted onto the base by Ben, while the gate guard gave him only a cursory glance after recognizing Ben. First, they drove past the beachside obstacle course with its menacing looking, three-story rope ladders and a series of beams resembling the wood apparatus used in women's gymnastics.

"You want to take a lap through this, Mark?" asked Ben with mock seriousness. With a chuckle, Mark responded, "Nah, I don't think so." "Ah, come on, you were a gymnast right? You can handle this." "Nice try, Ben, but that was thirty years ago, you know!"

Then they passed by the sand berms that rim the ocean where resolute men sit in long lines in the 60° surf, arms encircled, as they face the large breaking waves, roll in the sand and then launch into those five mile runs on the beach (all before breakfast).

The tour continued past the barracks and the dining hall, located roughly a mile from the beach, where the tired men are challenged to run again in order to save precious time to eat. Finally, Mark passed the deep pool building where SEALS are drown-proofed by swimming with shackled legs under water for a whole lap. Nearby stands the infamous "I quit bell", which a defeated man rings to signify his decision. The experience was a striking testament to the patriotic passion, the precisely structured training regimen and the laser discipline of the men who succeed this turmoil to put on the dress whites and don the gold Tri-dent pin of the Navy SEALS.

On this particular day, a new class of SEALS had just been awarded their Trident in the completion ceremony. A small group of these men were standing outside the building, their pristine posture signaling a distinctive readiness for action. They suddenly circled up to congratulate each other with a synchronized jump and chest bump, accompanied by a deep, vibrant Yoo-rah chant. Unlike the contrived pomp of any previous graduating ceremony Mark had ever attended, this moment was filled with a palpable, raw sense of pride. In the silent aftermath of that moment, Mark recognized the profound dedication and the heroism to come, when these men would deploy, as phrased in their unique vernacular; *down range.*

Recalling this humbling yet thrilling tour, the indelible image of our American military power and the personal dedication of the men and women who serve was frozen in his memory. Mark remains indebted to the graciousness of Ben and wishes him well in his future actions. Mark's own pride and gratitude to be an American were fully magnified by this experience.

CHAPTER 6.

Other Plans

"Life is what happens while making other plans."
John Lennon.

oday as Mark races toward seventy, thoughts of longevity creep into his mind (*only periodically of course!*) Many people over forty years of age claim that time speeds up in some inexorably perceived way as we age. This rings true for Mark as well. A fuller awareness of mortality resonates inside the psyche. Quoting Robert Plant of the band Led Zeppelin, "I hear the sound of time roaring past me. And there is no time to lose."[12] Clearly, this need not be considered as a morbid or pessimistic thought, but simply as a definite numeric reality. As we age the roaring is more audible. We realize that the number of past days outnumbers the projected number of future days (unless we become among the world's oldest humans).

With age and the accompanying altered perspectives, people change. The changes occur on many potential planes: mental, spiritual, intellectual and oh yes indeed, physical. In particular, the physical changes might be

---

[12] Durhan,Nancy. At 66, the Led Zeppelin frontman blazes an ever-evolving musical path. USA Today, Jan 19 2015

expressed by the term, *change-agetion*. The march of time seems to creep along quietly and unnoticed, inexorably arriving to the conscious attention, without fanfare. When questioning many older physical therapy patients about their primary functional or injury problems; Mark repeatedly heard the identical and imprecise declaration, "I'm old!" When the patients were asked to elaborate with the question: "Oh. Well, when did it happen?", the most common response was merely a puzzled frown and shrug of the shoulders.

Witness Mark's crew from his first college days at St. Cloud State. Although time and distance have separated them, they were able to arrange a most fascinating, informal reunion dinner in 2005. Set apart from the masses in a semi-private room at the downtown Minneapolis Thai restaurant, Sawatdee, the six guys and their wives enjoyed a great festive time of drinking, dining, stories and remembrances and a sudden, roundabout roasting of Mark and his college escapades. So much for nostalgic grace, or at least, selective memory! Yet the visible effects of *change-agetion* had taken effect on these once hopeful, active and unworried young men, that now stood smiling, yet slightly circumspect in their group picture. (Fig 6.1)

Although an individual may not feel equal to their chronologic age, to younger friends and colleagues, they automatically earn the label of "old school." Mark wears that label with pride. Joking that he is indeed old school, Mark quips: "I don't know the difference between tai chi and chi tea!" "When I started my career humans had abdominals, but now they have a core." When asked if he likes sushi, Mark replies, "Oh yeah, I take it home and grill it. (momentary pause for laughter). Hey, but seriously, someone at my home likes it. If I drop some on the floor, my dog rolls in it."

Harboring a clear and present disdain for rap music (rhymes with crap)and accepting the fact that twerking could well cause low back pain without much gain, yet Mark still sees the world continuing to turn. The inexorable change of plane operates at multiple levels. Being sensitive to the inevitable changes in musical preference between generations, it remains questionable if rap music will endure as time proceeds. Will there really be an expectation of a classic rap station twenty years from now, heralding the FM call letters like CRAP – Classic RAP at 94.2 on your dial?

As a by product of the long hours of providing clinical patient treatment, it became clear to Mark that his prescribed exercises became stale and lacked optimal effect if they were not spiced up with humor. Exercise is worthless if there is no willingness to move! But for a medical professional, the skillful use of humor to enhance exercise poses a definite precarious balance between professional distance and effective, motivational interaction. As a physical therapy educator, Mark was often asked to designate his most important tools to alleviate pain, restore physical function or athletic skill and thus provide effective rehabilitation. As his career morphed into the third decade, the answer clearly became "exercise and humor."

The notable author, Maya Angelou, expanded the essence of happiness to include laughter and humor. She claimed that she felt a lack of trust in those who did not laugh. Mark believes that also. However, in our current hypersensitive American socio-cultural mindset of political correctness at all costs, it is a big challenge to script and deliver jokes, screwball observations or offer situational humor without grievously offending someone. While it is generally obvious who that person might be, it is periodically a shocker, when no outward cues are evident. Ouch!! And while never reliant on the wisdom of former girlfriends who unceremoniously dumped him, Mark acknowledges the truth in one particular girl's quote, referenced in her cold letter of dismissal;

> *Humor is not humor,*
> *Unless it is shared and understood*
> *If not, it is a weapon.*

Gosh, can't people take a joke? reflects Mark. Perhaps not, considering the looming specters of lawsuits for defamation, derailment of promising careers from a single slip of the tongue(or brain) or immediate social rejection among the person's so-called friends and sponsors.

Historically, Abraham Lincoln (our vaunted sixteenth President and Mark's favorite) foreshadowed this cultural dilemma by adapting one of his famous quotations. By substituting the word *please* in place of his original *deceive,* we are warned as follows:

You can please all of the people part of the time, and part of the people all of the time, but you can not please all of the people all of the time !!!" Wow, those words are so heavy with impact and yet, light with being.

As an aside, we may consider Lincoln by many perspectives, not the least of which was his wisdom, his visionary thoughts and his eloquent words. For instance, it is astounding to consider that Lincoln scripted the words to the famed Gettysburg address while riding on the train from Washington to central PA and delivered the address with minimal sleep and apparently, no chance to rehearse the words or the necessary intended inflections.[13] This evidenced the mark of a truly astounding orator. Ironically, like many fine men to follow, President Lincoln died on April 15th! Death and taxes, baby

With age comes perspective. The physician/writer Sherwin Nuland [14] states that longevity is determined by a triad of C's: constitution, choice and chance. Considering this consummate idea; the perspectives that people adopt as they age are unarguably affected by all of those 3 C's, but the segment of choice shines through as the most critical.

Amazing examples of human achievements powered by the elements of courage, faith, positive thinking and iron clad, inner-most self confidence abound. These achievements extend across the far-reaching spheres of sports, war, coping with disease or disabilities and survival episodes. Consequently, we can visualize that it is not the event that is critical, but rather the mental and psychological reaction to the event. The individual's internal coping mechanism that is set to work in the aftermath, that is most the critical element.

For instance, Mark remembers his grandma's death as graphic evidence of the power of choice with the human condition. Mark's grandmother Myrtle (on his mother's side) lived to 104, despite suffering only a few minor

---

[13] Lubin, Martin.The Words of Abraham Lincoln. Speeches, Letters, Proclamations and Thoughts of the President Who abolished Slavery and Saved the Union. Black Dog& Leventhal Publishers. 2005.
[14] Nuland, Sherwin.2007. The Art of Aging. A Doctor's Prescription for Well-Being. Random House, NY.

medical issues, with exception of pronounced visual deficits from glaucoma; she had no hospitalizations and used no regular meds. Myrtle was quiet, small in stature (four foot eleven in.) but large is spirit and rarely complained about her health, or ailments. Poor Myrtle suffered frequent self-induced wounds to her hands and arms as she pursued her vital passion of raising roses. Pruning with poor visual focus is not a recommendable practice. During her last years, she began to worry that *the Lord had forgotten her* and she determined to rectify this by staunchly refusing any food and liquids for over a week and then passed away quietly.

Mark's father and all the males on that side– the grandfather and two uncles, lived to their early eighties with minimal medical issues and died fairly suddenly. Apparently then from a hereditary standpoint, Mark may have many more years to enjoy as he contends with this increasing pace of time passages. Rest assured however, that Mark is fully committed to regular, varied physical exercise. He has abandoned heavy competitive sports due to constraints of ageing on his joints and muscles, but still adheres to a mixture of running, golf, swimming, biking and occasional Frisbee throwing when someone else is available.

With age comes perspective: a quelling of radical untried constructs, a smoothing of mental rough edges and a quieting of the baser urges. When faced with a contest or physical conflict it may be that "backing off" is not merely resulting from a loss of strength or speed, poor vision or questionable balance, but rather a widening of wisdom and a shimmer of hope in a fonder future (coupled with the explicit realization that bones and ligaments heal much slower now and cause more pain along the way).

With age comes perspective. During a long career as a physical therapist and athletic trainer, lessons about the physical body and it's care are paramount. The constantly growing understanding of medicine, surgery, nutrition, genetics and exercise are impressive testaments to our scientific culture and our quest for quality of life. Expanding on Nuland's second element of longevity, the choice, truly exercise stands alone as the most singular, simple and inexpensive medicine available to mankind: for all cultures and nations, regardless of scientific advances or technologic advantages. Treading lightly, we can expand the idea that exercise can prevent and modify most diseases and dysfunctions.

Exercise may even cancel some conditions, or least eliminate the need for the pharmaceutical cascade that Americans are so often subjected to. Physical exercise demonstrates an elegance of economy for health care.

During Mark's first job as a physical therapist providing nursing home contracting (turn-key services for space allotment, equipment set-up, patient evaluation and rehabilitation, coordination of ancillary nursing services and appropriate Medicare and other insurance documentation—ugh, paperwork city) he encountered a very special, indelible patient case.

The patient we will call Helen, was an eighty-two year old lady who suffered from cardiac and lung dysfunction, She had relied on wheelchair mobility exclusively for over two years. During Mark's initial contract completion with every nursing home, each patient was evaluated for rehab potential and the individual patient goals were carefully considered in rehab planning.

During his initial discussion with Helen, Mark sensed her pride and excitement over her favorite grand-daughter's upcoming wedding, noting her wistful statement that "I would just love to be able to walk down that aisle for the wedding." Predicated on the physical assessment of Helen, Mark recognized an excellent rehabilitation potential. Her only primary deficit was weakness of her hip muscles and the obvious de-conditioning effects from the prolonged sitting. In addition, the nursing staff recognized her low motivation to work with them on standing and attempts to walk with a walker and manual assist.

"Well, Helen, why don't we get to work on your strength so you can walk down that aisle ? Think how wonderful that will be!" exclaimed Mark with an acquired vocal certainty that dissuaded doubt and allayed patient fears. "Do you really think I can?" scowled Helen, projecting that common level of doubt that often intersedes between an older seasoned adult and a young, vibrant and buoyant health professional offering suspect advice.

Ironically, this generational mistrust, is also manifested in the opposite direction. As referenced by Robert Gates, the former Secretary of the Defense Department in his book, Duty: Memoirs of a Secretary at War [15], "Young people are inherently skeptical if not cynical, about the rhetoric of older people and those in authority because too often their actions do not correspond ."

"Absolutely, you can. You'll have to work at it, though. You know, Rome wasn't built in a day. When is that wedding?" queried Mark. "Well, let's see, it's in about 6 weeks,

---

[15] Gates, Robert M. Duty: Memoirs of a Secretary at War. Alfred A Knopf, 2014.

now, I think." "Ok, Helen that's our timeline, then. We'll start your sessions tomorrow, OK?" M*ark thought, perfect, the amount of time was well within a reasonable time-line for the necessary strengthening, balance and gait training that was to ensue.* "Mark, I'll give it a try." conceded Helen softly, with minimal conviction, avoiding eye contact as she gazed at the floor.

But Helen gave spirited effort with the rehab and day by day she gained confidence and motivation with the exercise program. Remarkably, she even changed many of her resistant personality traits as reported by the nursing staff with their daily self-care interactions. Meanwhile, Helen's strength increased dramatically to include repetitions of partial squats with minimal stand-by assist, stair climbing, single leg balance of up to ten seconds and walking with only a stand-by assist for two sessions up to three-hundred feet by the fourth week of rehab progression.

At the end of the fourth week, Helen proclaimed with obvious pride and conviction, "I've talked to my son about the wedding and I know I can walk down that church aisle and the stairs, with his help. I am so pleased! I really can't believe that we've done this!" "You have made great strides, Helen, so let's keep going for this next week, to get your endurance up."

Wow, for the inexperienced new health professional, patient victories like this are powerful forces in building confidence. Both the learned skills from professional school as well as the impact of positive communication are reinforced. Additionally for Mark, the necessity of full commitment by the patient was demonstrated, as well as the succinct awareness about the time requirements for functional recovery. Yes, health professionals are people too, and like all humans, are bolstered by positive outcomes and happy clients. Well, certainly there is nothing new about this concept. The Bible offers the consummate reference for this in Colossians: *Encourage one another, build each other up.*[16]

People rarely ever boast about great plans that go bust, relationships that start promising only to end sourly, or can't miss stock purchases that explode into sudden, dramatic losses. But in Helen's case, a truly fantastic transformation had occurred and as a young clinician, Mark derived a great measure of personal satisfaction .

As planned, Helen attended the Saturday wedding and her son reported to the nursing staff how proud she was during the ceremony, how much she enjoyed the reception and how she glowed with all the attention during the entire day. Mark could barely wait until his scheduled Tuesday sessions at Helen's particular facility to get report about experience. After stopping at her room and noticing a made bed Mark checked in at the nursing station to ask," Where is Helen ?"

"Oh, Mark, ah, she's gone." came the quiet, hesitant reply. "What do mean?" Mark's concern was obvious, yet tinged with a rising disbelief. The nurse continued without hesitation, "She died yesterday morning.(a moment's pause) It's really sad, you know, she was so high after the wedding." Those words were truly an unexpected kick in the gut. Momentarily stunned by this news, Mark was lost in quiet contemplation. Fighting off that initial disbelief; Mark could merely utter, "Oh, that's too bad." Sensing Mark's shock, the nurse quickly added, "Yeah, she really worked hard for you, you know."

---

[16] Collosians 1:1-11.

Now a swelling of the imponderable realization surfaced. Helen had made the intrinsic choice that she would achieve one last, difficult, but very important goal and apparently that was her final, climatic wish. A pair of dramatic lessons had emerged from this case. First, the power of positive thinking propelled Helen's rehab progress. Secondly, she seemingly made a measured choice about prolonging her life and then presumably a conscious decision on the timing of death.

The application of effective physical rehab programs requires a set of skills, techniques and behavioral problem solving methods. These elements comprise what may be termed as "a professional toolbox", inclusive the precept of establishing a professional *distance* between the clinician and patient. Upon reflection of Helen's case, the wisdom of a professional distance was reinforced as a crucial element in Mark's ever-growing "toolbox". He realized that his emotional response to Helen's death had failed a professional standard.

With age comes perspective and when synthesized by a sensitive mind or spirit; over time a degree of wisdom may (or should) emerge. For a health professional, the concepts of wisdom, professionalism and expertise may become intertwined causing a blurring of their distinctions. But in the role of a post-graduate educator, Mark's awareness and his own expressions of these terms evolved as an acutely important issue. Sharing and savoring the curated wisdom of myriad fellow humans: authors, musicians, scientists, scholars, theologians and yes, occasionally even a selected politician; can pose a worthy use of our time and bestow a practical avenue for personal enrichment.

In fact, the mere essence of learning has been an innate pursuit of Mark's. Therefore, he relishes the counsel and wisdom of varied sources. For example, he has adopted the motto of St. Thomas University in St. Paul, MN. as a personal guideline.

Think Critically, Act Wisely and Work Skillfully.

In this vein, Mark's own personal life motto has generated from his love and respect for wise advise or a thoughtful message:

Learn something everyday from everyone.

Adherence to this motto enables the person to grow and mature each day, without standing in class registration lines, attending undesirable required courses or avoiding the heavy tuition costs. But at the very least, the motto allows you to avoid boredom, because each chance meeting or discussion with another person, offers the potential for a new idea.

Consider this: wisdom often flows from the common man, injected by their life's intense moments of victory or defeat, celebration or grieving; their distilled thoughts may provide a valuable guidance. Our society tends to overlook such truths, just as we may hastily pass the ragged homeless person on the curb. Hence, we may miss a deep and meaningful idea or a fresh approach to living.

Years ago while reading a scientific periodical, Mark paused to relish the definition of an expert, paraphrased as someone who can devise a plausible solution to a complex problem with minimal data and do it in a rapid, time compressed manner. This definition fits many of the therapeutic challenges in physical therapy and most probably, in the practice of medicine in general and for many business dilemmas. This definition dampens over-confidence and beckons self-examination with difficult patient cases or during traumatic life conditions.

This definition also offers more depth than the glib view that an expert is someone who travels more than one-hundred miles to a presentation with Power Point in tow.[17] It is more also more realistic than the humorous Holiday Inn Express television commercial that projects an expert as anyone who has spent a night at their hotel, because a good night's rest allows you to do anything!

(Admittedly, this funny tenet has provided years of good-natured reference during continuing education course presented by Mark.)

When considering the hotel's advertising slogan above; rest is essential to peak performance, but it is not the central ingredient for expertise or successful practice. In contrast to the requisite qualities of an expert, we can link a definition of the term, professional.

First of all, if we adopt the most minimal qualification, a professional is someone who is paid for a given work task. In the business world, a professional is often also licensed by a regulatory agency and/or has completed specialized training, a college degree or post-graduate work. Additionally, the definition may be expanded in a real-world, bottom line sense to portray a professional as someone who is having an off day in their service delivery, yet the client does not know it. The clients do not recognize any reduction of service quality nor do they notice any stressful change of behavior from the individual professional.

Not to diminish any heroic military missions or

---

[17] Personal communication: G.Davies, 1992.

common citizen's efforts to save people beset by accidental tragedies, but a shimmering example of professionalism was demonstrated by Michael Jordan in the 1997 NBA playoff finals with the Chicago Bulls. Suffering from an intense case of stomach flu that left him weak, dehydrated and suffering nausea before the game; Michael pressed on to help his team, scoring 38 points and making the winning three point shot in the final minutes of the game. While this may not have been the optimal decision for the player's health; his sacrifice and effort were tributes to his competitive will and team loyalty. After the fact, many experts considered this his finest game of a splendid career, if not the most heroic.

From a healthcare clinician's standpoint the elements of problem solving with physical ailments or injury are often a confusing challenge. At times, the standard treatment regimens may fail to address the subtleties of individual human variability. The clinician must ask, "Now what?" Herein, the concept of meta-cognition is beneficial. The term, meta-cognition encompasses the real time analysis of why an individual or health professional is thinking about, feeling or reacting to a specific stimuli in a certain way. Mark found meta-cognition to provide a sort of mental breath of fresh air and usually facilitated a more clear cut problem solving pathway.

Guided by years of experience in applying treatment models, Mark learned that a trial and error approach applied in a step-wise sequence is periodically required to answer that "Now what ?" question. When indicated, the trial and error process is streamlined by the use of the meta-cognition principle.

Applied to a wider scope of life conditions, Cullen Hightower [18] claimed; "Wisdom is what is left after running out of personal opinions." Through the repast of and the sandy riposte of a singular life-stream, we all may face a river of inattention driven only by the subconscious. But always we face the change of plane. The power of choice underlies our path. Owning the awareness that all of our choices are tethered by consequences, is to be forewarned and yes, wise. This awareness minimizes an individual's mistakes and the potential torment of regret, debt and self-doubt that may result from ill-advised choices.

Powered up by 5 Hour™ energy drinks, the majority of American masses remain under-read, sleep deprived, overweight and overfed and often disengaged in their work— seeking cell-phone salvation with tweeting, gaming and texting. For release, they may deposit themselves in seating with poor postures to watch mindless TV shows full of Hollywood blah. Ironically, these may be the very programs that stir the vilification of traditional, conservative religious groups for the decadent lifestyles that Hollywood shamelessly champions

Seemingly, the critical mass of modern writers focus on outlandish adventures and death-defying events, sexual exploits and plots with mystery, war and deceit. But these stories overlook the tick-tock of the average man's daily clock; the daily AM coffee to revive, a yearning anticipation of a lunch sandwich which leads to an excruciatingly delayed five o'clock whistle. And so another drab, unrelenting string of work days mercifully ends. Then the anticipated

---

[18] Kong Kam Fu, J. 2008. Whiplash: Associated Disorders: Myth and Controversies. Part 3. CME series, Hong Kong Medical Society.

joy of the weekend arrives, only to be steadily grounded by a weighty dread sensation that builds its momentum as Sunday wanes, and Monday beckons yet again. Is it any wonder that so many people long for the eventual refuge of retirement?

Mark contends that many careers in sports, business and the professions follow a similar path: contention to succeed, ascendance – if successful and decline if a glitch occurs (i.e., Tiger Woods hitting a tree, getting divorced and falling from golf grace). Finally, if progress and persistence pay off, an elective retirement may result. In the event that the elements of hard work, positive guidance and good fortune coalesce during the final work years, even a measure of transcendence may be present.

Underscored by 37 years of clinical physical therapy and sports medicine practice, Mark's patience with patients had waned and the essential satisfaction had dulled. As expressed by countless patients, their pain had become a pain. While burn-out is a compelling and critical issue for today's professionals, this was more of an out-lasting of work stimulation, an attitude that he was unwilling to endure more of the same. In brief terms, Mark's will had now become mostly, – won't. During one of the rare in-depth discussions with his father, Mark asked how he decided it was time to retire. Without hesitation, Mark's father quipped that when a person looked forward to a vacation for restoration but still felt depleted when returning to the work setting, it was time to close the curtain on that act of the play. This perspective was an important consideration for Mark's decision-making.

As aside to this idea, the quirks of the English language

offer an amusing paradox. In common terms, when someone returns from a great vacation, they are thought to be refreshed and rejuvenated. Mark has known many people who are fresh, but has never heard anyone describe themselves as "*juvenated.*" In fact, the dictionary doesn't even recognize it as a viable word.

Interestingly, retirement was a common current theme for multitudes of other so-called baby boomers, like Mark. According to statistics culled by the US Dept. of Labor, Mark's retirement year in 2012 occurred in good company, because 2.1 million other folks made the same decision in a single month! That is an incredible fact, emphasizing the importance of the social security system payouts to a huge number of American citizens.

When Mark's choice to retire was finalized, there was no measure of disrespect of his chosen professions nor any regret about the important accomplishments and experiences that he had accrued. Furthermore, there was no lingering burden that he had not achieved enough or had failed to explore any promising career opportunities. Rather, he was tied to a peaceful air of completion and the assurance that this change of plane would manifest new perspectives and new joys. Mark realizes that achieving any level of transcendence has yet to develop. However, Mark's life has followed a carefully constructed and satisfying plan. Thanks, Mr. Lennon, for the heads-up precaution.

And thus we have arrived at a crossroads with Mark, a sort of collision of narratives and memoir, an excursion through past travels, travails and triumphs His events were guided by hard work, an enterprising search for fulfillment, rich blessings and that trusty old SSS –self sustaining spirit. With each new welcomed morning sunrise; Mark avoids willful and harmfully provocative words and those screamed with wild regrettable emotions. Instead he chooses to stay moderate and central in behavior and to travel mid-way between destiny and decision. Ah, such a fantastic change of plane!

As the expanse of time has unraveled for Mark, his time has been touched gently by the hand of God, led by benizens of good fortune and giving mentors (both personal and professional) and driven by the SSS. In hindsight, perhaps the SSS was actually a subconscious communiqué with God. As the moments of our daily events unfold into the future to become our history, our own personal narrative, we all remain caught in that life current toward our shared final, ultimate, astral and spectral change of plane.

ACKNOWLEDGEMENTS

While it is impossible to mention everyone that has contributed to the inception and completion of this book, nevertheless, it is imperative that I herald a few. First of all, to my parents who instilled a love of reading and a respect for thought prior to action.

To a high school friend, Peter Scherrer whose off-the-cuff comments gave me confidence in my own intellect.

I must make special mention of my many mentors: Drs. Joe Wilkes, Tom Branch and Sam Reber and to fellow colleagues: the late Gordon Cummings and late John Allison, as well as George Davies and Bruce Greenfield, Bill McDonald and Jay Shoop.

I value the immeasurable insights of the patients and athletes who have entrusted their recoveries to me and to the coaches who inspired both discipline and humility. Finally, in those rare moments of creative outbursts of words, phrases and ideas; my dear wife, Clella, graciously afforded me intellectual space and private time to "get it done!" Thanks to you all.

ABOUT THE AUTHOR

Albert Marks graduated from the University of Minnesota. He is a clinical specialist in physical therapy and athletic training and has founded several private practice physical therapy facilities in three states. His writings include research papers, scientific textbooks, scientific journal editorials, and a book of poetry. Marks lives in Atlanta, Georgia.

Printed in the United States
By Bookmasters